D0513771

THE SALES MANAGER'S GUIDE TO TRAINING AND DEVELOPING YOUR TEAM

THE SALES MANAGER'S GUIDE TO TRAINING AND DEVELOPING YOUR TEAM

National Society of Sales Training Executives

Edited by
Raymond A. Higgins
Sales Training Consultant

NATIONAL SOCIETY OF SALES TRAINING EXECUTIVES
Sanford, FL 32771

BUSINESS ONE IRWIN
Homewood, IL 60430

This publication is designed to provide accurate and
authoritative information in regard to the subject matter
covered. It is sold with the understanding that neither the
author nor the publisher is engaged in rendering legal, accounting,
or other professional service. If legal advice or other expert
assistance is required, the services of a competent
professional person should be sought.

*From a Declaration of Principles jointly adopted by a Committee
of the American Bar Association and a Committee of Publishers.*

Sponsoring editor: Cynthia A. Zigmund
Project editor: Susan Trentacosti
Production manager: Bette K. Ittersagen
Jacket designer: Image House, Inc.
Compositor: The Wheetley Company, Inc.
Typeface: 11/13 Palatino
Printer: Book Press, Inc.

Library of Congress Cataloging-in-Publication Data

The Sales manager's guide to training and developing your team /
    National Society of Sales Training Executives; edited by Raymond A.
    Higgins.
        p.   cm.
    Rev. and updated ed. of: The sales manager as a trainer / by the
National Society of Sales Training Executives. 1977.
    Includes index.
    ISBN 1-55623-652-2
    1. Sales executives—Training of.   2. Sales management.
I. Higgins, Raymond A.   II. National Society of Sales Training
Executives.   III. Sales manager as a trainer.
HF5439.8.N37   1993
658.3'1243—dc20   92–11933

Preface

Preparing this book was a humbling experience because the advice comes from *so many* successful sales managers, sales trainers, and trainers of sales managers, most of whom are past and present members of the National Society of Sales Training Executives. Picking the best from 50 years of corporate North America's sales and management trainers has made me seek the most effective way to organize the ideas for a field sales manager's use. I decided to stick with a framework that has worked for me in the past.

Thirty-five years ago I began using a framework of 'exercises' which involved the manager-participants' real-life problems in Managers' Workshops on "Getting Work Done Through People"—workshops that have provided hands-on training for thousands of managers in a variety of industries. These exercises required practice of about **a dozen skills that can make or break managers in achieving results through sales personnel:** making the adjustment from selling to managing salespeople; mutually setting clear goals; managing time; solving people-problems; recruiting and selecting salespeople; teaching a task; coaching; reinforcing performance; questioning and listening; conducting group meetings; goal-planning discussions; and self-development. Managers who fine-tuned these basic skills, without exception, got better results through their subordinates. Perhaps it was the combination of being forced to *practice* the laws of the human environment on the participants' own managerial problems that changed their attitudes toward management. Improving all three basic factors: attitude (desire), skill (practice), and knowledge (know-how)—are key to managing others.

Since May of 1987, trainers from the National Society of Sales Training Executives have used the same concepts to improve those dozen skills in intensive three-day NSSTE sales managers' workshops for newly appointed managers.

If you are a field sales manager seeking guidance on what you *must know and do* to get results from your salespeople, this book is for you!

If you are a recently promoted salesperson now responsible for managing other salespersons, this book will help you get results through your salespeople, avoid the mistakes commonly made by the newly appointed sales manager, and reach your sales goals.

By implementing the guidelines presented throughout the book you should be able to prevent the loss of your top performing sales representatives, manage your time more effectively, manage the frustrations often associated with the sales manager's position, maintain control, and prevent declining sales.

If you are an experienced sales manager, this book will also help you get better results through your salespeople; avoid those mistakes you haven't yet experienced, and meet your sales objectives by a wider margin.

Learning from Experience

Most of what we learn we learn from what we *do*. As a sales manager (whether brand new or experienced) you would not gain much from a book that gives little more than "nice to know" material—or one that doesn't show "how." On the other hand, you can't rely solely on learning from "the school of hard knocks" for two reasons: (1) Good guidelines are essential; we miss too many "lessons" in experience; and (2) Mistakes in "managing" are far more costly than "selling" errors. When your career path turned from selling to managing, you *had to* change to the "Trial and Success" technique of learning (to manage) *because you could no longer afford "Trial and Error"*! Managers must benefit from others' experience.

Can managers also improve from reading a book? The answer is "yes" if the readers practice and critique the methods shown in these skill areas. To fully gain the benefits of the book, you will need to absorb, change, and *apply* Attitudes, Skills, and Knowledge. Knowing what to do is easier than developing the skill to accomplish the objectives set forth for you. Therefore, this book asks you questions, provides tools to adapt and use in your job, and challenges you with checklists to help you meet higher standards of performance as a manager.

Where This Book Came From

In 1975, 21 North American corporate sales training directors (all of whom were also members of the National Society of Sales Training Executives) wrote chapters for the original book *The Sales Manager As a Trainer* (edited by Jared F. Harrison of General Electric Company). When the book became outdated, I . . . as one of the original authors . . . was asked to revise it. You are reading the result. The former NSSTE book logically organized subjects for managing sales training including the following chapters: "Determining Sales-Training Needs," "Planning for Sales Training," "Sales Training in the Field," "Sales Skills Training," and "Evaluating Field Sales Training Programs." The book presented "sales training" as an activity separate and removed from every day supervision which it should not be! In the previous edition, many of the ideas from the authors concerned training in the classroom (which represents a tiny part of the field sales manager's training opportunities). *Training* does not stand alone: it *is a part of your continuing efforts in getting the job done through your sales representatives.* Good training saves the manager time. This new book hopefully will show you how in a simple and straightforward fashion.

What Is in This Book

Using much of the original book's best ideas, I reorganized it so that the chapters center around basic guidelines for implementing a dozen "skill" areas; the same framework that proved so successful in NSSTE's manager training workshops. This book allows you, alone or with a group, to participate, learn, and fine-tune these field sales management skills:

Skill 1. JOB UNDERSTANDING (Overview of the Manager's Job)
Skill 2. GOALS (How to Set Standards)
Skill 3. TIME (How to Manage it)
Skill 4. PROBLEMS (How Do I Solve Them?)
Skill 5. SELECTION (How to Recruit and Select Trainables)
Skill 6. TRAINING (How to Teach a Task)
Skill 7. COACHING (Keeping Reps On Track)
Skill 8. REINFORCEMENT (Getting Them to Do it)
Skill 9. QUESTIONING/LISTENING (Skills for Understanding)

Skill 10. GROUP COACHING (Getting Participation in Meetings)
Skill 11. EVALUATING (Helping, Not Telling)
Skill 12. SELF-DEVELOPMENT (Summary and Manager Check-
    list)
TRAINING RESOURCES (Where to Find Them)
ADDENDUM (Forms)

You can get additional help in *NSSTE Sales Success Booklets* on these specific HOW TO subjects: "Create Effective Sales Training"; "Recruit, Interview, and Select Productive Sales Reps"; "Orient New Sales Representatives"; "Critique your own Sales Call"; "Manage Time and Territory"; "Manage your Key Accounts"; and "Get Participation in Sales Meetings", and in the *NSSTE book:* "Selling Through Negotiation" (write: NSSTE, 203 E. Third St., Sanford, FL 32771–1803 or call: (800) 752–7613.

ACKNOWLEDGMENTS

I am indebted to Jared F. Harrison who did a yeoman-like job of editing the original book. The credit for this new book belongs rightfully with the professional trainers who contributed their ideas and thoughts; to Roger Turnquist, Chairman of the NSSTE Publications Committee who encouraged me to create an entirely new book; and with the forward-thinking Board of Directors of NSSTE who approved its publication. Two chapters from the original book, revised by their authors, appear as separate chapters in these new Guidelines: Chapter 12, "Summary: How to Develop Yourself" by Charlie Herrmann and Chapter 13, "Where to Find Training Resources" by Richard S. Miller. To some of the other chapter authors' tips, I have added ideas and experience culled from NSSTE Editorials, hundreds of Managers' Workshops, Sales Sucess Booklets, and manager training material of dozens of additional NSSTE members who have trained sales managers in their companies. From NSSTE Editorials: Bob Whyte's "Commandments To Newly Appointed Sales Managers" (Chapter 1); Chris Suffolk's "Time Management" (Chapter 3); and Charles W. Kraft's "Positive Reinforcement in Employee Training" (Chapter 8). Donald B. Waite's research results ("Help me, Don't tell me!") augment several chapters. I used some of John H. Rose'

NSSTE Booklet in Chapter 5. Chapter 10 includes several pages of Homer Smith's material from NSSTE's earlier book. The other chapters were written by this editor (Raymond A. Higgins). I am especially indebted to Walter R. Mahler (WRM Inc., Wycoff, New Jersey) who was my early mentor and shared with me the teaching of "Seminars on Coaching and Appraisal." The "Five Developmental Principles," basics of "Understanding the Job," and "Coaching Check List" were adapted from Walt's teachings. Also included were ideas and exerpts from NSSTE Editorials by John H. Burns, James F. Evered, F. William Heil, Russell S. Manthy, and Judith C. Quinn.

I apologize to the many NSSTE members whose original how-to's (reported throughout this book) must go unidentified for reasons of space and failing memory. I hope I have, meanwhile, preserved the best ideas of the 21 chapter authors and Jared Harrison who prepared the original NSSTE book, *The Sales Manager as a Trainer.*

Raymond A. Higgins
Editor

National Society of Sales Training Executives

The National Society of Sales Training Executives (NSSTE, 203 E. Third St., Sanford, FL 32771) is committed to improving sales, marketing, and customer relations through excellence in training. The Society was founded in Cleveland, Ohio, in 1940 to create a medium (a network of corporate sales trainers) for better results from training effort and budget. During World War II, NSSTE played a valuable role in the exchange of ideas for production training. Immediately after the war, NSSTE aided the U.S. and Canada in economic development and returned to concentrating on sales training. In recent years, NSSTE broadened the focus to include the entire field of marketing education. Membership is limited to persons who manage the function which has the responsibility for training sales and marketing personnel. Each member must submit an editorial each year, belong to an official committee, and attend at least one semiannual meeting every year just to retain membership.

About the Editor

Raymond A. Higgins is a management training consultant based in Phoenix, Arizona. Ray began his career selling door-to-door and operating his own business while attending college. In 1950 he moved into training as Assistant Professor at Michigan State University. He served as Director of Education during 11 years at Super Market Institute (now Food Marketing Institute) and 25 years at The Dial Corporation as Director of Sales Training. Ray has authored hundreds of management guides, handbooks, and editorials; personally trained more than 3,000 managers in executive development workshops; and conducted sales training for thousands of sales representatives. A member of the National Society of Sales Training Executives since 1973, his editorials have won three "Gold," three "Silver," and three "Honor" awards. Ray pioneered the "Bedlam Practice" and "Grinder Practice" training methods now used by many sales trainers. Ray Higgins authored a chapter in the first NSSTE book *The Sales Manager as a Trainer,* served on the NSSTE Board of Directors, and developed the format of NSSTE's very popular Sales Managers' Workshops. His previous book is the historical novel *From Hiroshima, with Love,* a documentary on the rebuilding of Japan. During World War II Ray served as navigator on a B-24 bomber crew. His B.S. and M.S. degrees are from Ohio State University.

About the Chapter Authors

Chapter 1 Robert Whyte, Vice President—Marketing for the Porter Henry & Co., Inc. of New York, has been a sales and sales management trainer for 40 years, having started as a "Fuller Brush Man." A member of NSSTE since 1969, Bob has been awarded 10 medals for the excellence of his editorial contributions, several of which concerned the Plateaued Salesperson.

Chapter 3 Christopher M. Suffolk is Sales Training Program Manager for The Dial Corporation, Phoenix, Arizona, where he is responsible for the development and execution of sales and sales management training. Chris authored "How To Manage Time" in an award-winning 1991 NSSTE editorial. His experience includes a variety of consumer products, field sales, and sales management positions.

Chapter 8 Charles W. Kraft of Morris Plains, New Jersey, recently retired as Director, Sales/Management Training for Warner Lambert Co. C.H.P.G. of Morris Plains, New Jersey. A NSSTE member for 16 years, his 1991 award-winning editorial "Positive Reinforcement in Employee Training" is used in this chapter.

Chapter 12 Charlie Herrmann, president of Speeches Unlimited, Owatonna, Minnesota, is one of America's most popular humorists, seminar instructors, and motivational speakers. Formerly a vice president of Josten's, the recognition awards company, Charlie has been a member of NSSTE since 1964. A co-author of the book *The Sales Manager As Trainer,* his contribution is the summary chapter of this book.

Chapter 13   Richard S. Miller, Manager of Training & Conference Services for MSD AGVET Division of Merck & Co., Inc., Rahway, New Jersey, has been with Merck since 1970. He has conducted training courses in more than 20 countries around the world. He earned B.A. and M.B.A. degrees at Cornell University, gained selling experience with Sealtest Foods, and became that organization's first Sales Training Director. He is a Past-President of the National Society of Sales Training Executives and is a recipient of the James R. Ball Memorial Award in recognition of leadership contributions with the American Society for Training and Development.

Contents

Chapter Ten
HOW TO CONDUCT EFFECTIVE SALES MEETINGS 115

Chapter One

Overview of the Sales Manager's Job

When you got the news that you were moving into management, you probably relished the challenge, basked in the "congratulations," and felt elated. If you received the usual management training, your advance was made by what we call "The Knighthood Method":

> I dub thee Field Sales Manager. Go forth into the world and manage. Don't ask me what thee is supposed to do—or how to do it—but thee better do it well!

You are now a sales manager. You and you alone are accountable for the performance of your salespeople. You select or help select them, supervise, coach, and counsel them, and you try to motivate and train them. Although your company may help you by providing formalized training programs, in the final analysis it is you, the sales manager, who must provide the day-to-day training and development experiences. If you look closely at your job description, you will most likely find a statement such as: "responsible for the continuous training and development of field salespeople." Naturally, your final evaluation will depend on bottom line results, but if you have done a good job in training your people, the bottom line will take care of itself.

You know how to sell. Your outstanding sales ability no doubt led, in part, to your selection as sales manager. You assume that that sales experience will help you in straightening out the district you've been assigned. Maybe you've already run into a problem . . . perhaps one of your sales reps is not selling as much, or as well, as you'd like; or selling the way you did. If you are lucky—really lucky—someone has already told you that successful, outstanding sales representatives can fail miserably (or succeed gloriously) as managers of other sales representatives. For guidance you've turned to this book. You want to be the best manager you can be. You are willing to try new ideas, change your outlook, improve your people skills.

Your new job is two-fold: (1) managing the business; and (2) managing your people to get that business. Your district may be too big for you to do all, or a majority, of the selling. Now your success depends on your staff. Chances are managing the business doesn't worry you, it's the people. Now you must manage and develop sales reps to grow that business, manage them to achieve this year's goals, and develop them so your company has qualified people to keep it in business into the foreseeable future. By managing both the business and your staff successfully, you can also be successful and hopefully move up.

BASIC GUIDELINES FOR THE NEW SALES MANAGER

There is a stereotype of the brand new field sales manager. This stereotypical sales manager frequently sees him/herself as "Supersalesperson" and initially goes through the district like a whirlwind, grabbing the bag madly from the sales reps to let them see with their own eyes what a hotshot salesperson he or she is . . . the manager who often feels absolutely compelled to rescue his/her sales rep halfway through almost every sales call. He/she is also the manager who sometimes lets the new charges know who's the new boss, that "things are going to be different from now on!" Although these examples may sound exaggerated, they occur time and time again.

The new manager can also be the direct opposite of the take charge type. Even though he/she may have great potential, the new manager can start out being timid, uncertain, and unprepared to fill an aching leadership void that may have existed for a long time. He/she wants to get off on the right foot, but doesn't really know how, and is crying out for guidance.

Whether the new field sales manager is a bull in a china shop or a shrinking violet, the result is often the same—a demoralized and alienated group of salespeople. The tragedy is that the damage done on that very first "go-round" may take years to heal. I recall some years ago receiving several phone calls from sales reps I had previously trained who were in a state of shock over some unbelievably stupid things said and done by a newly appointed and as yet untrained district manager. At the time I conducted a three-week program each year for new sales managers, but the next one wasn't scheduled for several months. By the time that particular manager came in for formal training, he and his reps were barely speaking. He had lost two outstanding producers and several others were actively job hunting. He never succeeded in digging himself out of the hole he had dug for himself.

The "New Sales Manager Syndrome" kept popping up year after year and was a constant frustration to me. The fact is that newly appointed managers are thrust into a gigantic vacuum and, lacking formal training in what the management process is all about, some fill it the only way they know; by continuing to sell— or by being hardnosed and authoritarian. Being directive seems to come naturally to most of us!

If you see yourself in any part of this stereotype, you must change instantly! In due course of time, most new managers calm down, but the damage they can do to their people and, most of all, to themselves by the time they get formal training is sometimes incalculable. The fault is the system's, not theirs. Management skills are not God given or transmitted by osmosis. The point we frequently overlook is that the field sales manager's initial meeting with each of his or her reps is unquestionably the most important get-together they will ever have. If it turns out to be a disaster, you can't turn back the clock!

How can you avoid the mistakes of the stereotypical sales manager? Start by following these eight guidelines.

1. Manage others so that they get the job done—don't do it yourself. While you were promoted because, among other things, you established that you are a superior salesperson, that was not the prime reason for your promotion. There is no need for you to prove to your sales reps that you can outsell them! Such a course of action is also fraught with danger, because you could very well find that there are some who are better sales reps than you are. If selling ability was the only criterion for promotion, they may have been promoted rather than you!

2. You should, on your first swing through the district, decline any offer to carry the bag. This could also save you the embarrassment of being "set-up" to sell the meanest S.O.B. in the territory! You're out there to see and learn, not sell!

3. Above all, resist the temptation to jump in and 'rescue' any of your reps who—in your opinion—are either not doing a very good selling job, or actually appear to be losing the sale. Discuss the call in detail with your local rep and agree upon your role (if any) during the call *prior* to the call. If he or she can handle it without major assistance—or any assistance—from you, so much the better! However, if the visit is to a key account and the annual contract or an equally critical issue is being lost, you should be prepared to assist with a suggested solution.

4. Observe. One of your goals, on the first swing around the district, is to begin to get a fix on the strengths and weaknesses of all your people. That is simply not going to be possible if you make a lot of the calls or take over during the presentation. Painful as it may be, at times, concentrate on observing.

5. Your primary objective, on that first visit, should be to learn all about your people—and to begin to develop a genuine trust relationship with each one of them. To foster this you should say—about two minutes after you meet them—"On this visit, I'm here primarily:

- To get to know you.
- To learn all about you and your family.
- To find out what your goals are.
- To learn about this territory and how things are going here.
- To find out about any difficulties you may be having.
- To get the benefit of any ideas you may have and, above all, *to learn how I can be of help to you.*"

Let the rep do the talking; there's plenty of time later on for you to talk.

6. You might not reject or refuse to listen to opinions offered about your people by a former manager, a regional manager or others—but bear in mind that these salespeople now work for you, and any decisions or actions you take with them should be based on your personal observations and conclusions. Wipe the slate clean! If you accept at face value some highly negative criticism of one of your people, you enter upon your new relationship with a built-in bias that could well have the effect of causing a self-fulfilling prophecy.

The best way to avoid being hung-up on someone else's views is to devote your first swing through the territory to observing, asking questions, listening, and making your own judgments.

7. Learn to recognize that 'vibes' and 'personal chemistry' are important and will play a definite role in your relationships with your people. You will undoubtedly have better vibes with some of your people than with others. That's to be expected. However, just because you don't hit it off initially with one rep as easily as with another doesn't mean that the latter may not be an outstanding performer. In fact, he or she may turn out to be your top performer.

8. Your people all have different personalities, styles, and interests, and it is your job to judge them on performance, on results; not on whether they act, talk, think, or sell the way you do! Each individual develops uniquely in his or her own world. In growing, each of us takes on bits and pieces of knowledge, attitudes, and skills. As one becomes more and more expert in selling, he or she becomes more and more different from others. Those things that made you successful in selling (aggressiveness, persistance, closing skills, habits of working alone, personal knowledge, and the desire to win) may be of no use to you as a manager unless you can acquire the ability to stimulate and bring forth sales results from others. You must foster within yourself the ability to teach, train, and coach. This ability to get results through others is often harmed by use of "sales pressure," the dishing out of advice and exhortation. Yet, some of your selling skills will serve you well. The key skills of understanding different people and selling consultatively, will help. Remember, though, to recognize the *differences* between selling and managing.

APPLYING WHAT YOU ALREADY KNOW ABOUT MANAGEMENT

You already know a great deal about what is good management. If you were promoted to management from the ranks of sales rep, you have your own experiences of working under the supervision of several managers: teachers in school, parents, straw bosses, group leaders, supervisors, and district sales managers. Without doubt, some of those experiences may have helped you grow, learn, and improve. In other instances you may have felt dead-ended or discouraged; you marked time, felt you were inhibited from developing, or that your time was being wasted.

By thinking about these experiences (both good and bad), you can learn what's important about leadership.

The following two questions—"Who was the best manager you ever had?" and "What specifically did he or she do that makes you say that that manager was the best?"—have been asked of thousands of managers. NSSTE Trainers compiled responses from District Manager Workshop participants over many years. All descriptions of what the best managers did are included in these five actions:

1. Helped me know what was expected.
2. Gave me the chance to perform.
3. Let me know how I was doing.
4. Gave me the assistance when and as I needed it.
5. Rewarded (or punished) me for performance.

Individual responses to *"What things my best manager did that helped me develop"* included "Enthusiastic—challenged me"; "Gave 'stroking'—both written and verbal"; "Honest—let me know where I stood"; "Trusted me"; "Gave responsibility"; "Stood behind me, right or wrong"; "Showed HOW"; "Pushed me to do better"; "Managed by example"; "Let me make decisions"; "Had the answers"; "Allowed mistakes"; "Firm but fair"; "Showed confidence in me"; "Explained, showed me how, let me do it"; "Consistent in praise"; "Gave me the credit"; "Encouraged, a good teacher, kept me informed." Write your responses on the "Best Manager/Worst Manager" sheet in Figure 1-1.

FIGURE 1–1
Things Done by My

Best Manager:	Worst Manager:

Thousands of responses to the "Best Manager" question all boiled down to the five Developmental Principles listed above. Violate any of these in managing your people and you inhibit development, you get less than optimum results, and you are likely to lose good people!

When you examine negative work experiences, the same five principles emerge as missing. Look back at your own unpleasant experiences—jobs where you felt dead-ended, your development inhibited, like quitting if you could. Do you remember what your "worst" manager did? In most cases, "poor" managers applied the opposite of the five principles . . . "unclear, inconsistent on what he/she expected, kept butting in and taking over, insincere, failed to encourage or correct, no help or guidance on how to do it, never heard from (except to get blasted!)"—yet, that worst manager "took all the credit for any successes." You "felt more rewarded by getting away from the work." What did your "worst" manager say or do that makes you remember them as "worst"?

CHECKLIST

_____ Learn to manage and let your sales staff sell.

_____ Decline any offer to carry the bag.

_____ Don't jump in to rescue a rep.

_____ Assess the strengths and weaknesses of your people by observing.

_____ Begin to develop a trust relationship with your people and listen.

_____ Listen to the opinions of a former manager, but act on your own observations and conclusions.

_____ You will like some of your reps more than others. Your best performer may turn out to be one you don't "hit it off with."

_____ Judge your people on performance results, not on whether they act, talk, think, or sell the way you do.

_____ Set for yourself high standards of performance, strict principles of conduct and responsibility, and respect for the individual and his/her work.

Chapter Two

How to Set Clear Goals

You and each member of your team need a realistic understanding of what's expected in the job. Clearly understood objectives help each team member toward self-management and self-improvement. In this chapter you will learn how to clarify your own job objectives and how to inform your staff of what's expected from them. Tools and techniques suggested here will help you implement self-management by objectives (SMBO), the process of management that produces winning teams. Let's start with your job.

UNDERSTANDING YOUR JOB AS SALES MANAGER

Remembering what your "best" manager and "worst" manager did may direct your attention to your current situation as a manager of others. Right now you may want clarification of your job and the probable expectations of your own manager. For newly appointed managers this need for clarification often is of crisis proportions. All of us have some need of the first of the five Developmental Principles discussed in Chapter 1: *"know what is expected."*

If your boss has been too busy to answer all your questions about your accountabilities, don't panic. Get a start now on what you think your standards should be.

Job understanding is another way of stating the first coaching principle: providing knowledge of what is expected. You need two questions answered: *what is the job to be done?* including the responsibilities and, (even more important), *what is a well done job?* What is your accountability for results and the degree to which specific results must be achieved?

Both questions need answers! And while the first can be explained pretty much from your job (or position) description, the answers to the second question usually requires person-to-person discussions with your boss. Your boss provided you a written job description document. It may say something like this:

1. Plans and organizes . . .
2. Communicates effectively approved sales plans . . .
3. Supervises sales personnel assigned to the District . . .

But after reading it, you still feel unsure of yourself in your position of sales manager. If you don't know exactly what is a satisfactory performance for each of your responsibilities, you need to define the missing standards so you can go over them with your manager. Here are three steps to help you get started.

THREE STEPS FOR DEVELOPING GOALS OR STANDARDS

A three-step process is best for developing specific standards of performance for a job. A helpful format is shown on the following pages with an example partially completed for the sales manager. The three steps are:

1. MAJOR RESULT AREAS (RESPONSIBILITIES)	2. MEASURES OF PERFORMANCE (INDICATORS)	3. STANDARDS OF PERFORMANCE (GOALS)
→	→	

To apply the process to your own job, follow these steps.

Step One: Think of the major result areas of your job such as sales (budget) accomplishment, key account development, trained (adequate) personnel, district coverage, district expense control, reports and records, company property, and so on. These job responsibilities are often implied in the job description. They may be stated as activities ("Plans . . . ," "Initiates . . . ," "Supervises . . .") rather than end results. To put them into a more useful working job description format, list them as *nouns*. Naming the responsibility using a noun puts a firm handle on it that all can understand. Listing activities only increases vagueness and misunderstanding. Be sure to include all your *major* responsibilities.

combining different result areas and qualifying adjectives. List the most important results first, then check them with your boss.

Step Two: Don't stop at knowing the boss's priorities! You also need to know how he or she evaluates each responsibility and the specifics of his or her expectations. What are the factors to be considered in determining when your position as sales manager is done well? How is your performance measured? What is used as evidence of results? So, for each responsibility, list the indicators of performance (measures). Identify *several* things which indicate how well the job has been done. Ask yourself: "What things must my boss take into account in determining when a job is well done?" These indicators of performance are the evidence, or a measure, of performance that is precise, time-sensitive (per week, per month), and stated in measurable terms. With your boss's list of job measurements (the names of the measures), you're on your way to knowing what is expected.

Step Three: Set specific standards. What are the exact results required, the degree of performance that is "satisfactory" (how many dollars, units, sales per week, expenses under what percent of sales)? In other words, what are the end results supposed to look like? What are the specific *goals*? These standards or goals are usually expressed in numbers, time and/or tolerances. Good standards follow the SMART formula:

Specific.
Measurable or Observable.
Attainable.
Realistic.
Time sensitive.

A suggestion: You and your boss agree upon what represents reasonable performance and what represents outstanding performance.

Figure 2–1 shows a partial example of a sales manager's Responsibilities, Indicators, and Standards of Performance.

Of course, your manager has already assigned budgets and some other standards to you. But you need all important goals written for easy reference. Listing specifics for every responsibility and checking them with your supervisor is a giant step toward understanding. This listing gives you a clear picture of your whole job.

FIGURE 2–1
Field Sales Manager's Goals (incomplete)

Responsibilities	Standard of Performance	
Indicators of Performance	Reasonable	Outstanding
1. *SALES VOLUME*		
a. $ volume per period	$975,000	$1,100,000+
b. Number of cases sold	25,000 cs.	29,000 cs.
c. $ volume as % of budgeted $	100%	100% +
d. Number of budgets made	6	All
e. Trend: $ this year versus year ago	+ inflation	+ 10%
f. District rank in region	Top half	Top third
g. Share of market, Nielsen %	17%	18% +
2. *KEY ACCOUNTS DEVELOPMENT*		
a. No. new placements/quarter	3	4+
b. Dollar Volume	$560,000	$630,000
c. Distribution gains versus losses	balance	+ 2
d. % overall distribution	87%	93%+
3. *TRAINED DISTRICT STAFF*		
a. No. making budgets	4 of 5	All
b. Competency, current jobs	satis. progress	1–2 promotable
c. No. days work/withs	2/mo. or +	no one missed
d. Morale—turnover	satisfactory	noticeably +
e. No. calls/day/rep	7.2	8 +
4. *COST OF SALES*		
a. District exp. as % sales	3.9%	3.6 or – %
b. Sample expense	$xxx	$xx
c. Auto and travel costs	and so on	

Why not get a pencil right now and work up your own Responsibilities-Indicators-Goals (R-I-Gs) as shown in Figure 2–2? By investing as little as a half hour thinking about what you want your boss to take into account when he reviews your performance can pay huge dividends. Take your preliminary worksheet to your supervisor and get the corrected standards. (You of course will have to change the examples used here to fit your job's responsibilities, the measures or indicators that are available to you in your company, and the specific standards to which you and your supervisor agree.)

FIGURE 2–2

Worksheet for My Job as Sales Manager

Responsibility	Indicator of Performance	Standard of Performance	
Major result areas.	How performance is measured.	Define end results which represent adequate and outstanding perf. levels.	
		Reasonable	*Outstanding*

SALES

a) _____ _____ _____
b) _____ _____ _____
c) _____ _____ _____

KEY ACCOUNT DEVELOPMENT

a) _____ _____ _____
b) _____ _____ _____
c) _____ _____ _____

TRAINED STAFF

a) _____ _____ _____
b) _____ _____ _____
c) _____ _____ _____

DISTRICT/MARKET COVERAGE

a) _____ _____ _____
b) _____ _____ _____
c) _____ _____ _____

COST CONTROL

a) _____ _____ _____
b) _____ _____ _____
c) _____ _____ _____

RECORDS and REPORTS

a) _____ _____ _____
b) _____ _____ _____
c) _____ _____ _____

COMPANY PROPERTY

a) _____ _____ _____
b) _____ _____ _____
c) _____ _____ _____

SELF DEVELOPMENT

a) _____ _____ _____
b) _____ _____ _____
c) _____ _____ _____

With agreement on your standards of performance (or goals) between you and your regional manager, you gain a better understanding of your job as a sales manager. Writing down your goals enables you to:

1. Focus daily efforts toward real achievement and perform your job without a lot of supervision.
2. Measure your own progress against your goals.
3. Be specific when seeking help or direction.
4. Periodically review your progress (with your regional manager) and reset goals.

GOALS—ASSIGNED OR MUTUALLY DEVELOPED?

You know what your district's sales budgets, allowable sales expenses, and district objectives are. (If you've acted on the above advice and prepared R-I-Gs for your job you have a very exact knowledge of district goals.) You have probably already apportioned in your mind a share of each district goal to specific sales representatives.

Let's say you have been doing your homework and have a definite idea of what is a realistic goal for each rep. Before finalizing anything check for further input from these important sources: your own manager, previously set goals, available data sources, and the sales representative him/herself. We cannot stress enough: *Get the input of the sales rep concerned.* While it is necessary to split up the quotas that will achieve company objectives, you and your salesperson are the best people to tell if a goal is realistic and how best to achieve that goal.

TO BUILD A TOP TEAM: LET YOUR SALES REPS KNOW WHAT'S EXPECTED

The difference between employees who perform well and those who perform poorly is determined by how they are treated. As a sales manager, your high expectations, high standards of performance, and faith in your staff to meet those expectations can translate into high performance on their part; a sort of self-fulfilling prophesy.

High performing work units, in study after study, are shown to be led by managers who are positive role models.

But it doesn't just happen by magic or accident: you can't just wish high performance and have it happen. Your staff respond to the way you treat them. If you listen and communicate expectations clearly, allow them to risk performance, give guidance and help when and as it is needed, communicate progress in specific terms, and reward on the basis of results, your team will respond favorably. Since you are judged by what your staff produces, your rewards are greatest when you do these five things skillfully.

WHAT DO SALES REPS WANT?

Like the sales manager, sales reps want to know what is expected of them and whether they are meeting those expectations.

One firm, Sales Staff Surveys, Inc., makes it a business to help sales management listen to what their sales reps say. Twenty-five thousand sales reps were asked questions about their managers and their responses were reported by President Don Waite in the booklet: "Help me, Don't tell me!" (Sales Staff Surveys, Inc., 30 Main St., Danbury, CT 06810). Answers included:

"There is confusion about direction and objectives."

"District goals are not clear to me."

"I need to know what we are trying to achieve and the strategy to get there."

"I'm uncertain as to just where my district manager wants me to spend my time."

To the question "What ONE thing would you institute or change to improve your sales effectiveness?", one rep replied: "Field managers should become more results-oriented rather than activities-oriented. They should be trying to increase sales through motivation and positive feedback instead of Gestapo methods and

intimidation." Another sales rep answered: "Business would ex-
plode if we were managed with POSITIVE rather than negative
reinforcement!"

ALL BEHAVIOR IS CAUSED!

We affect our relationships with others; our relationships affect
us. (One wit defined human relations as "treating people more
like humans and less like Relations!") On a more serious note, we
can define the "A-B-C's of Human Relations" as: All Behavior is
Caused! Sales reps' behavior is caused by their perception of how
they are treated. As a sales manager, you can affect their perception of this treatment through the following: the climate of your
supervision; the output you expect; the input of your help; the
feedback on progress you provide and rewards that come from
performance. For positive results from your sales representatives,
you must implement ALL Five Developmental Principles.

Practice Results-Oriented Management

If your treatment of reps is objective and results-oriented, you will
get best productivity and they will be satisfied. You will also have
little difficulty moving to a management process that might be
called self-management by objectives (SMBO).

SMBO teaches one to have a high regard for responsibility and
initiative. For the manager this means the responsibility for performance is put upon the employee. While you are still accountable
for the rep's results, your energies can then be spent on evaluation, review, teaching, coaching, team leadership, and analysis.
This requires of you a dispassionate, nondirective, patient behavior, in short, to have faith in your staff and faith in your ability to
help their job understanding and productivity.

Cooperative planning is essential to results management. Mutual understanding of job responsibilities, indicators, and goals is
peculiar to SMBO. Did the process of writing down your
Responsibilities-Indicators-Goals help you understand the goals
of your own managerial job? You may be thinking about how to

apply responsibilities → indicators → goals to your staff. Nothing you do as a manager will have greater impact than to clarify for each sales representative what is expected!

HOW TO HELP SALES REPS GAIN JOB UNDERSTANDING

How do you get your sales reps to stay on top of their jobs when everything keeps changing? Today's buyers are more sophisticated, better trained, better informed, and more computer literate than ever before. You have a recurring problem in providing knowledge of what is expected because jobs, markets, and sales reps change. By reviewing quarterly with each staff member his/her Responsibility-Indicator-Goal list, you solve those problems. If the sales rep has taken on a new responsibility, you can add the new responsibility with indicators and goals to the document. As the job changes, the list changes. Quarterly goals can be set and accepted. Problem areas can be discussed, causes understood, and action plans developed.

Set goals together. Don't impose them on your reps. To gain most from the goal list, you and your sales rep must develop jointly his/her written list of responsibilities, indicators, and goals and use it as a constant reference point. Let's look at some examples.

Here are a few typical lists of sales rep responsibilities:

Consumer Prod. Sales	Pharmaceutical Sales	Industrial Sales
Retail/wholesale sales	Sales volume	Sales volume
Store conditions	Phys' script habits	New accounts
Coverage	Store/hosp. cover'g	Contracts
Expense control	Informed customers	Expense control
Co. property	Drug sample invent.	Factory liaison
Records/reports	Administration	Reports and records
Personal development	Professionalism	Personal growth

You decide to meet separately with each rep to discuss the rep's goals, the strategy for accomplishing the goals, and to get com-

FIGURE 2–3   Partial Example
Sales Representative's "Working Job Description"

Responsibility	Indicator of Performance	Standard of Performance	
		Reasonable	Outstanding
A. SALES	Cases sold/day	150 cs./day	250 cs./day
	Displays sold/day	4 displays	5 displays
	% of budgeted cases	95 %	100 % +
B. DISTRI-BUTION	Number items/account	12	15
	New placements versus lost	+ 1 per day	+ 2.5/day
	New accounts opened/mo.	1	2
C. RETAIL COVERAGE	Calls per day	7.1	9
	% of Plan	89 %	96 % or +
	Top 80 missed/4 wk.	5	4 or fewer
D. EXPENSE CONTROL	$ per mo.	$ xxx	$ xxx
	Company car expense	always s.s. gas	
	Phone	within $ xx average	
E. COMPANY PROPERTY	Auto condition	Maint./wash/vac.wkly	
	Sample cs. & equipt.	Weekly orgnzd-up to date	
	Display POP	3 per store	5 per store
F. RECORDS & REPORTS	Accurate coll. of data	Regularly & accurately	
	Transmit hand-held	as sched.	File maint.
	Competitive activity	2 per mo.	3 or more
	Up-to-date'ns of call cds.	Reviewed/4 wks	2 wks
G. PERSONAL DEVELOP'T	Prof. societies/activities	Membership	Officer
	Self-study	up to date	Subsc. trade

mittment to accomplishment. You might approach the rep with a statement something like this:

> Joan, to help both of us get a clearer idea of your territory's objectives, I want us to share, and agree on, what kind of results we are after. Take sales for example; as measured by units sold, what number do you think you will be able to hit by next closing period?

If the rep protests that the new goal is too high and you can't adjust it downward, tell the truth:

> I'm sorry, Joan, but that's what we've got to get from your territory in order to make district budget. . . . What might we do in order to assure that you make that number before the close?

Together, you might develop a list as shown in Figure 2–3. Periodic up-dating of each sales rep's list is easy when needed.

Benefits of Preparing Goal Lists

Benefits of mutually developing and using objectives lists are many:

- Sales reps receive direction and are encouraged to meet agreed to goals with little direct supervision.
- Clarifies who is responsible for what.
- Provides a basis for periodic review of progress.
- Aids individuals in his or her self-development efforts.
- Facilitates breaking in a new sales rep.
- Permits establishment of value or level of a job.

You can see from the partial examples shown earlier in this chapter (pg. 18) that some numbers do exist for judging qualitatively. Customer comments, your day-to-day observations, and recording of critical incidents bring realism to the measurement.

In consumer sales, you may want to prepare a separate list of "Store Quality Standards" (see Agway example, Figure 2–4).

PLAN AND EXECUTE

When the two of you have set, listed, and agreed upon the sales rep's goals (through discussion of Responsibilities, Indicators, and Goals), turn the discussion to plans for accomplishment. Review with the rep those goals that will be most difficult to achieve, why difficult (what's causing the difficulty), and discuss possible actions to help accomplishment. Then, get agreement on a specific plan of action: who will do what, when, and, how you will help. After your initial goal setting session has demonstrated how you arrive at goals, you can pass on to the rep the responsibility to initiate the process when new goals are needed.

A Performance Contract

Responsibility for maintenance of the goal list can be placed upon the subordinate, preferably after you give instruction in preparing the document. What you develop is, in effect, a performance contract. You and the salesperson you supervise agree on specific

FIGURE 2–4
Agway Store Quality Standards

A. CUSTOMER SERVICE

- Employees know what is advertised and where in the store the merchandise is located.
- Employees are identified via Agway uniforms.
- Telephone is answered by the third ring with a friendly greeting, store name, and employee name.
- Customers entering the store receive a customer oriented sales approach, including a friendly greeting.

B. CUSTOMER FLOW

- Customers are encouraged to circulate throughout the store.
- Customers can easily find items that they are looking for.
- Customers have easy access to all items on display.
- Store aisles are well marked and clear of obstructions including merchandise.
- Customers can pay for their purchases quickly and conveniently.

C. MERCHANDISE PRESENTATION

- The store looks well stocked, no core items out of stock.
- Departments are clearly identified.
- Each department faces on the main traffic aisle.
- Each department is introduced by a feature display.
- Key departments occupy the prime floor space.
- Feature items are prominently displayed.
- Customers can easily find the current price of any item they might purchase.
- Merchandise is displayed utilizing the vertical concept.
- Merchandise is clean and dust free.
- Like items are displayed together.
- Displays emphasize impulse and add on sales items.
- Close-out items are presented in a special display.
- Shelf items are properly faced, giving the impression assortments are complete.
- Feature displays are current with the season.
- Impulse items are featured at the sales counter without obstructing customer flow.

D. INTERIOR GRAPHICS

- Store signs are clear, attractive, preferably machine produced.
- Store hours are conveniently posted.
- Every department is well identified with an easy to spot sign.
- Every item being promoted is identified with a sign to add excitement and reinforce the promotion.
- Signs are used to promote both price and value.

goals or standards of performance. These agreed to standards are written down, a copy is kept by each party of the agreement, and you and the sales rep can use it as reference points. These written goals help as guides in day-to-day supervisory contacts. And the field contacts (work withs, phone discussions, paper and electronic exchanges) permit you to make notes and plans anticipating the next periodic coaching (or goal setting) interview. That way, you can up-date the goals when necessary. You can be more realistic in setting goals that require reasonable stretching to reach.

Once you have worked through goals and gained the sales rep's confidence, you must keep the process on-going: review the list periodically (never less than once every six months) so each rep's working job description keeps pace with changes in the position.

Figure 2–5 is a blank form for developing goals. Use the format to work up written standards of performance (goals) with *each* sales rep. Schedule a time to sit down and mutually develop his/her most important responsibilities, indicators, and goals. On your work sheet, lightly pencil in the responsibilities, indicators, and goals you plan to suggest. Then negotiate a performance contract that helps everybody win.

CHECKLIST

_____ Does each of your sales representatives have a clear understanding of the job to be done?

_____ Does each rep consider the same part of the job to be most important as you do?

_____ Does each rep know for sure what you look at (take into account) in determining how well the job is done?

_____ Does he or she know exactly *what* results you expect, accomplished by *when*?

_____ Can you say, honestly, that you set specific goals for each sales representative under your supervision and that each understands those goals assigned?

_____ Do you keep these goals up to date?

_____ Do the goals set require some stretching to reach?

FIGURE 2–5
R-I-G Worksheet (to develop Standards)

Responsibility	Indicator of Performance	Standard of Performance	
		Reasonable	*Outstanding*
1.	a) _____	_____	_____
	b) _____	_____	_____
	c) _____	_____	_____
2.	a) _____	_____	_____
	b) _____	_____	_____
	c) _____	_____	_____
3.	a) _____	_____	_____
	b) _____	_____	_____
	c) _____	_____	_____
4.	a) _____	_____	_____
	b) _____	_____	_____
	c) _____	_____	_____
5.	a) _____	_____	_____
	b) _____	_____	_____
	c) _____	_____	_____
6.	a) _____	_____	_____
	b) _____	_____	_____
	c) _____	_____	_____
7.	a) _____	_____	_____
	b) _____	_____	_____
	c) _____	_____	_____
8.	a) _____	_____	_____
	b) _____	_____	_____
	c) _____	_____	_____
9.	a) _____	_____	_____
	b) _____	_____	_____
	c) _____	_____	_____

Chapter Three

How to Manage Time

Ralph, a friend of mine, seems to be one of the luckiest people I know. In fact, he just recently came into an unusual inheritance of a large sum of money. Terms of the inheritance are such that every day at 12:01 A.M., $1,440.00 is automatically deposited into Ralph's checking account. This money can be used in any way he wants; it can be invested wisely or simply squandered away without much thought or planning.

This inheritance is not without set terms and conditions, however:

1. By 8:00 A.M., $480.00 is automatically deducted.
2. Each subsequent hour, an additional $60.00 is deducted.
3. There can be no balance at the end of the day; the account must return to zero.

If you were Ralph, what would you do?

You wouldn't sleep late, or wait until 12:01 to decide how the funds are to be used. Instead, you would begin the day before, planning exactly how the funds will be spent . . . transfer some to stock, put a down payment on a boat, buy a new computer? Failure to plan how your money will be spent at 12:01 A.M. would result in lost money, something most people work hard to avoid.

This inheritance example serves as a good beginning to discuss time management, because like Ralph, every day each of us has 1,440 minutes automatically deposited daily into our "life checking account." We, too, have terms and conditions: by 8 A.M., 480 minutes have been automatically withdrawn, we lose 60 minutes each hour, and our balance returns to zero at the end of the day.

For most of us, though, when we talk of money, we are very deliberate in our actions. No one would fail to plan in advance their use of the inheritance, yet how many of us fail to take a hard look at how we use our time? The irony is that money lost can be remade, but time that is lost or wasted can never be returned!

The purpose of this chapter is to provide you with a process by which you can manage time. Although critical during your transition from sales representative to sales manager, what is presented here will be of value to you every day of your life, allowing you to make the most of all the time you are given.

> "Our clock of time is wound but once in our lifetime, to tick away 'til the energy, wound into life's spring at birth, runs out. No one of us knows when his or her mainspring will expire and the final 'tick' of life's clock will come, never to run again. Therefore: live, love and cherish each moment to the fullest—investing the talents and energy given you by the Almighty in the betterment of mankind—and be thankful for each tick of life's clock." (from invocation by William A. Kane.)

THREE STEPS TO BETTER TIME MANAGEMENT

Peter Drucker, a well-known author on business and management, has an interesting comment about time and planning in his book *The Effective Executive.* He says:

> "Effective executives, in my observation, do not start (planning) with their tasks. They start with their time. And they do not start out with planning. They start by finding out where their time actually goes. Then they attempt to manage their time to cut back unproductive demands on their time. Finally, they consolidate their 'discretionary' time into the largest possible continuing units. This three-step process:
>
> - recording time,
> - managing time,
> - consolidating time
>
> is the foundation of executive effectiveness."

This is excellent advice. If you stop and think about managing time, one thing stands out clearly: managing time does not involve *doing* as much as it involves *thinking*. To manage our time we must plan our time.

Let's look at each of these three steps as a means to better manage time.

Step One: Record Time

Before you can make changes in your daily activities (or in the ways in which you accomplish these activities) in hopes of better managing time, you need to reflect on, and record, where you are currently spending your time. Once you know where your time has been going, you are then able to assess if you are making the best use of your time and are in position to direct where you want it to go.

To accomplish this step, Figure 3–1 provides a weekly recap to keep track of how time is spent. As necessary, adapt the recap form to your position and industry. Time that you spend on areas other than those listed should be included under "Other." At the conclusion of the week, convert time spent to a percent of total time worked. Areas of time you might survey include:

1. Meetings with management.
2. Planning.
3. Driving/Traveling.
4. Reading bulletins-mail.
5. Writing reports/paperwork.
6. Telephone communications.
7. Recruiting sales personnel.
8. Other "overhead."
9. District meetings.
10. Training new sales reps.
11. Coaching, face-to-face.
12. Auditing reps/standards.
13. Joint sales calls.
14. Performance appraisals.
15. Other "supervision."

Completing a time survey like this is often eye-opening, frequently creating many questions to address. Once completed, analyze. Ask yourself:

- "Are there any facets of my job which I am not performing—from my customers', employees', and supervisor's perspective—that I should be?" If so, list these areas. To

FIGURE 3–1
Survey of Time Usage

Type of Activity	Mon.	Tues.	Wed.	Thur.	Fri.	Total	
1. MEETINGS w/management						Hrs.*	%**
2. PLANNING							
3. DRIVING/ TRAVELING							
4. READING bulletins-mail							
5. WRITING reports/paperwk.							
6. TELEPHONE communications							
7. RECRUITING sales pers.							
8. OTHER "overhead"							

"Overhead" Subtotal: _____hrs. _____%

9. DISTRICT MEETINGS							
10. TRAINING new sales reps							
11. COACHING, face-to-face							
12. AUDITING reps/standards							
13. JOINT SALES CALLS							
14. PERFORMANCE APPRAISALS							
15. OTHER "supervision"							

"Supervision" Subtotal: _____hrs. _____%

*Round to nearest .5 (half) hr.   **% = $\frac{Hrs}{Gr.\ Tot.\ Hrs.}$ Gr. Total: _____hrs.   100 %

ensure realism, these questions should be answered with supervisor, employee, and customer input.

- "Am I satisfied with current allocation of time spent on 'administrative/overhead' areas versus 'actual supervision'?" If not, identify where you would like to spend more time.

This may bring to mind some guiding considerations, like: "Is what I'm doing contributing toward my objective as a manager?"; "Will these actions contribute to the company?"; "Am I providing a value-added service in my action?"; "Am I improving relations with my sales reps and customers?"; Have I done what I need to stimulate rep development?".

Step Two: Managing Time

Once you know where your time goes and have addressed where it should go, ask yourself the following:

If I am to spend time performing functions which I previously did not do, or, if I am to spend more time on an area of my job than in the past, how will this be achieved without working an extra five hours each day?

This latter question is answered through Step 2, managing time. This process consists of reviewing where you spend your time and then cutting back on unproductive demands on your time.

For example, after reviewing the time recap prepared in Step 1, you note that an inordinate amount of time is being spent on overhead-type activities. Although these activities are important, you would like to allocate more time to actual supervision of your people. To achieve this, you want to reduce the amount of time spent on the telephone and time spent conducting district meetings. In managing your time, your goal is to look for ways to reduce both telephone and meeting time.

- To reduce telephone time, you note that time could be saved if both you and your sales personnel were better prepared for the call. To make better use of telephone time, you initiate use of a telephone planner by district sales reps and yourself (see Figure 3–2). This planner is designed to minimize idle conversation, reduce the need for callbacks due to omitted discussion, and accommodate post call notes for follow-up.

FIGURE 3–2
Telephone Planner for _____
date

Person/Number	Key Points	Results/Notes for Follow-Up	Done

- In recent district meetings, you note significant time is wasted because attendees stroll in late. You conclude that personnel have developed a casual attitude towards your meetings. After all, they never start on time, so why should they be on time (you regrettably conclude this attitude is not totally unwarranted given the precedent you've allowed in previous meetings).
Additionally, you determine that meetings start slowly as it takes time for everyone to get informed on the meeting's topics before productive discussion can take place.
To minimize unproductive meeting time, you decide to implement the following: first, all meetings will start and end on time. Secondly, attendees will be issued a meeting agenda in advance, everyone attending will be informed on the purpose of the meeting and all will be expected to bring asked-for materials and contribute.

Can you think of better ways to manage overhead time usage? Time saved as a result of your management effort can be reallocated to actual supervision of sales representatives, consistent with your time management plan. Can you improve supervision time?

Step Three: Consolidating Time

It is not uncommon to encounter brief periods of time which by themselves make it difficult to accomplish a task. Consolidating time refers to organizing your schedule in order to take those brief periods of 5 and 10 minutes and consolidate them into continuous periods of time, say 15 minutes, a time more conducive to completing a task.

This may not always be possible or practical to achieve. In situations where it is not within your control to consolidate time, those minutes still should not be wasted. Like a bank account, you can "deposit" accomplishment of small parts of big jobs by using those brief periods of time to: get out needed data, read some background material, call to set up an appointment, brainstorm a few minutes, just anything that moves the big priority project along. For example, it may be out of your control to be kept waiting by your boss for an appointment. You do, however, have control of how you choose to spend the time waiting.

A good rule of thumb is to expect to be kept waiting at some point in your day. Keep tasks with you such as reading materials or parts of a larger job that you can work on to move that project forward.

THINK ABOUT HOW YOU SPEND YOUR TIME

The process reviewed here—record, manage, and consolidate— has been presented and used by over 1,500 sales managers within the grocery industry. Does this process work? Absolutely! But only after each manager accepts one key element on time management:

> Time management is a mental process requiring more thought than action.

For many, this is difficult to grasp. Why? Our society expects managers to be busy, always on the move, making quick decisions. This is expected. After all, they are managers, a corporation's elite.

But the fact is, time management requires one to reflect on how time has been spent, consider ways to cut back on unproductive demands, and to analyze how time may be combined to form larger chunks of time conducive to accomplishing a task. These are all things that involve thinking, a mental process. To use two cliché's, time management is "doing the right things correctly," and "working smarter, not just harder."

Show me a successful, happy, sales manager and I'll show you an effective time manager. Make time your friend, not your foe. Record, manage, and consolidate.

Don't waste your time. Like my friend, Ralph, start thinking about a better time management plan now!

TIPS FOR HELPING YOUR SALES REPRESENTATIVES MANAGE THEIR TIME

The same process you are using—recording, managing, and consolidating time—works equally well for your sales representatives. Here is what Robert C. Immel lists as tips to help sales reps save time:

1. Take time to save time.
   a. On Monday morning or, preferably, Friday afternoon, list the five most important tasks to be accomplished during the week; decide which should be done first; then tackle and complete it.
2. First things first.
   a. Concentrate on a few things, and do them well.
   b. Identify the objective or result desired; eliminate things which don't contribute to that objective.
3. Telephone tactics.
   a. If possible, consolidate telephone time by allocating one or two time periods during the day to make or receive calls.
   b. When making calls, prepare by jotting down notes about what you want to say or find out during the call, and take notes during the conversation.
4. Try to minimize or avoid interruptions. You can be too available.
5. Do your best to make appointments that you set or participate in as productive as possible.
   a. If possible, push for specific solutions or answers—even if it's not your original objective. This will reduce the need for further calls.
   b. In approaching your manager with a problem, think it through first and come with your recommendation.
6. Delegate effectively.
   a. Don't do it yourself—the first time or the second time (if you have a retail merchandiser or someone to delegate to). Delegation multiplies your effectiveness.
7. Improve your decision-making capacity.
   a. Don't delay; that wastes too much time.
   b. Get the necessary facts, identify causes, possible actions, consider consequences, then decide and act.
8. Learn to say "no." Avoid making commitments you'd really prefer not to make or meet.

As their manager, you can help your salespeople to recognize and overcome weaknesses in planning and organizing. Most people are aware of their shortcomings, yet fail to do anything about them. To help, work with them to develop areas in which they are weak. If those areas are planning and organization, teach them to record, manage, and consolidate their time for better time management.

CHECKLIST

_____ Do you plan the use of your time in advance knowing that time lost can never be regained?

_____ Conduct an audit of how you currently spend your time.

_____ Cut back on the unproductive aspects of your job.

_____ Let your sales reps perform on their own. Delegate without abdicating by putting the proper balance on the amount of supervision given.

_____ Encourage your reps to bring you their recommendations instead of their problems.

_____ Do you delegate without abdicating by putting the proper balance on the amount of supervision given?

Chapter Four

How to Solve Problems

If a sales manager can better manage his/her time by reflecting on how time has been spent, considering ways to cut back on unproductive demands, and analyzing how time may be used to accomplish the right task correctly, would improving these skills help in managing everything? Reflect. Consider. Analyze. All things that involve thinking—a mental process.

How do we "think"? Do we identify the source of problems and analyze all options for correction while basing our decisions on factual documented evidence rather than emotion or conjecture? How do our minds work?

The surprising answer is that when we are faced with something that is going wrong, our minds are conditioned to look for quick answers, to jump to conclusions, or to make a decision without really thinking at all! The mind does not always work the way it ought to. This is OK with minor problems, but not with your managerial matters. Other people are involved now. The stakes are big. Your success hinges on the way you make decisions that affect your sales people and your company; and, on the way you involve your sales staff in helping you to solve problems in your area.

How do you solve problems and make decisions? Can you improve your decision-thinking? Can you learn to use proactive thinking?

You can't always prevent your mind from jumping to conclusions. Whenever you see something that is wrong it is natural to think: "What should I do about it?". Since you can't always stop your mind from making conclusions without having all the facts, you can become aware of the way you react and hold your fire until you analyze the situation to determine causes and evaluate appropriate solutions.

THE SCIENTIFIC METHOD

If you felt ill and went to the doctor, you'd certainly consider suing for malpractice if the doctor prescribed a powerful drug or operated without first asking you where it hurts. All good physicians carefully diagnose the illness before prescribing medication or surgery.

Let me illustrate the steps involved in the physician's scientific method:

Step 1. Subjective and objective analysis.
    a. What does the patient say? What are the symptoms?
    b. What do tests/examination show? What is the cause?

Step 2. Identify the disease.

Step 3. What are the possible treatments?
    a. Classify these treatments in order of effectiveness.
    b. Study the patient benefits and potential adverse reactions of each.

Step 4. Recommend and administer the most appropriate treatment.

Managers, too, pay a price for malpractice. A snap decision may destroy a relationship, cost future sales, or result in the loss of your best sales rep; so use patience when faced with important problems. The delayed response is the first sign of intelligence. Never lose your temper with a subordinate.

Some managers in the Western world have difficulty doing this. Not so with our counterparts from Asia with whom we compete. In Japan, managers shun making quick decisions, while politely agreeing to "look into the problem." Then the manager taps the opinions and ideas of subordinates and superiors and studies the potential consequences of each action before arriving at a conclusion.

Can a Sales Manager Learn from How Others Make Decisions?

After living 20 years in Japan, my father advised me in 1965:

"The best thing I've learned from working with the Japanese is patience. They seem to take forever to reach a decision. They'll stall and procrastinate and study the problem again. They share the problem

FIGURE 4–1
An Opportunity/Something Is Going Wrong

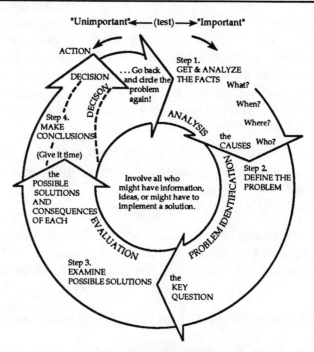

with all levels, discuss it all up and down the organization . . . but the decision is eventually made and the work gets done . . . and usually the result is better than we Americans would have done."

As a sales manager, he used his understanding of Japanese thought-processes to sell his American company's product to a 70 percent share of the Japanese market. I came back from visiting him in Japan with a better understanding of how a sales manager can solve problems: Why not combine the patient, cooperative techniques of the Japanese with the diagnostic, scientific approach to thinking and teach this process in manager workshops?[1]

Here is the process of problem solving that merges the scientific and Japanese styles of management. The four steps of analysis, identification, evaluation, and decision need to each be thoroughly thought through in a cyclical manner. A pro-active manager will consciously and deliberately think his or her way, clockwise, around the circle of steps several times before reaching a final decision and taking action (see Figure 4–1).

Discipline your mind to avoid the natural counter-clockwise jump directly to Step 4—Decision, except on the unimportant or minor problems. In the course of a day, you are bombarded with decisions to make; where should you start? One rep calls asking if you can meet a half mile from the location you planned; another requests a small change in his/her next day's route; what concession to make with an account?; how to cover the empty territory?; or where to grab a quick lunch?. When something is going wrong we need to first identify if we have a real problem and prioritize it. Three quick tests tell us if it is important:

Time—Will a solution matter a year from now?
Cost—Does it involve more than $xx (your benchmark for trivial cost)?
People—Could a decision hurt anyone?

If the answer to any of these is "yes," you have a potentially important problem that deserves patience and careful analysis. If a "no" response applies to all three, the quicker you decide the better!

A Step-by-Step Method to Solving Problems

Step One: Analysis—identify causes. The first step in solving a problem is to get all the facts, to separate facts from opinion, and to analyze the facts for identification of primary causes of the problem. Facts are information that doesn't disappear when you ask "why?", "how do I know?", "did I observe it with my own eyes or confirm it?". But don't ignore opinions ("I think this sales job is becoming a paperwork jungle!") as they can be helpful in suggesting where to look for more facts. Sharing important problems with your sales staff is a sign of strength. You get useful information and ideas. Besides, several minds working on a problem usually improves quality and almost always gains buy-in to decisions. Then simply separate facts from opinion and analyze the facts for cause.

Analysis of each fact is made from four key angles: the What, the When, the Where, and the Who. For example, you find that even your most seasoned veterans (the Who) are not reporting certain information (the What), even though it has been required for years (the When). Analyzing facts tells you that they all had been submitting it properly (had the skills) a long time ago. Is retraining needed (premature solution)?

Why have your veterans stopped submitting reports? Maybe they only had half as many items to sell back when they were taking time to properly complete the requested form. Perhaps they saw the use made of the information was more important to them then than now. They had a paper copy of the information and it helped in their planning the next day's calls. Now they put the data into the lap-top computer, transmit, and don't see it again. Analysis of When-it-was-not-a-problem reveals: (1) They knew it was expected and required. (2) They were allowed (had time and resources) to do it. (3) They had been shown how. Their manager helped them understand why and how. (4) They were able to track themselves and were informed of how they were doing. (5) There was something in it for them.

Change as a Cause. Most problems are caused by some change—something or someone or some priority has changed. Change is inevitable. You can't fight it. You can't deny it. You can't ignore it. Since change often results in problems, you are wise to look for change. Look also for differences in the What, When, Where, and Who, present when the problem is noticeable and absent when everything is all right. These differences point to cause. Pin-point the causes of the deficiency, and you can define the real problem.

Step Two: Problem identification—define the real problem. After considering and identifying the primary causes, define the real problem, the key question.

A problem well-stated is only half-solved! A precise and analytical definition from the standpoint of the What, When, Where and Who should be stated impersonally and in a single sentence (if at all possible). Stating a problem impersonally means telling what business objective is at stake.

The missing reports example presented above might be defined something like this:

The problem: Information vital to marketing is not being transmitted by all sales reps (all territories) since change to electronic

FIGURE 4–2

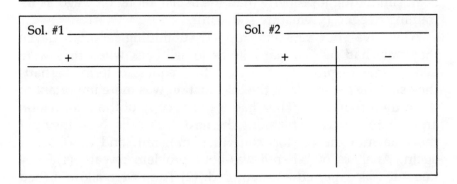

means; may be due to sales job priorities and perceived lack of benefit; no feedback of information and its uses, no hard copy, no consequences for noncompliance. How do we get full compliance?"

Step Three: Evaluation—consider possible solutions. Do you ever brainstorm? In a moment's time, you might come up with 15 or 20 possible actions. Jot them down as they occur to you. Many of them might be impractical, but chances are you'll see a germ of something usable in even the wildest idea. Something could prove useful that you would never have thought of when using critical judgment! So, with your list of alternatives, you can go back and cross out the unworkable, narrowing the possibilities down to a half-dozen of the most promising solutions. Never be satisfied until you have considered at least three possible solutions to any human problem! Most of the time you can create solutions that turn change into an opportunity.

List the pros and cons for each possible solution. Set up a "Balance Sheet" for each possible solution listing all the possible advantages and disadvantages for that solution. Do this for each possible solution on a separate piece of paper as illustrated in Figure 4–2.

Small, note-size scraps of paper are all you need for these comparisons. On each, simply jot the solution across the top, draw a large "T" and list the advantages in one column and the disadvantages in the other. Keep your mind open. Don't try to force any premature conclusions! Search out evidence on all sides of the question. Every solution has some advantages and some disadvantages. By recognizing and writing down all the possibilities using this method, you can compare advantages to disadvantages. Evaluating the probable consequences of each action helps you to avoid creating new problems with a rushed solution to this problem. Have you overlooked anything of importance to solving the problem? Circle the problem again. Is the definition the right one? Are any other solutions viable? How will people react? What is the probability of success for each action? Can you use combinations of the suggested solutions? A sequence of other solutions if your first choice fails?

Give Yourself Time. The human mind is an amazing organ. Hundreds of times more powerful than a computer, its billions of cells work best when it is not being pushed or pressured. You make your best decisions by feeding your mind with data—spreading out all the completed balance sheets to review them—and setting a deadline (ahead) when you will need a decision . . . say, by eight o'clock tomorrow morning. Then, get away from the problem and go on to another matter. Don't pressure yourself into an immediate decision on an important matter!

By setting a deadline a few hours ahead, your subconscious mind can work on it while you are performing other tasks. The answer will often come to you when you least expect it, usually when you are resting, combing your hair, or even walking the dog at night.

Remember, change is an opportunity. It can be a motivating dynamic. It can be planned on, understood, incorporated into a sales plan. Change can be a dependable aid in increasing sales effectiveness.

Step Four: Decision—decide! Weigh the evidence. Consider both pros and cons (consequences) of possible solutions. Then select the best, or best combination of solutions. It's often possible to combine the best of two or more alternatives, in ways that avoid possible disadvantages of each. Which remedy will give the most result for the least effort? Once you make a decision, be satisfied that you have made the best selection. Put it to work.

Implement Your Choice and Gain Acceptance.   Be sure to involve those affected by your decision. Sales reps care when they share. If you alone must decide, at least share discussion (and get ideas) of how best your reps can carry out the decision. Whenever practical, share analysis of district problems with your reps. Ask for their input and cooperation. To repeat: Involving subordinates in the decision-making process is a sign of strength in the leader, not weakness. Many minds focused on a problem will produce better solutions than your's alone.

Thinking proactively each time you encounter trouble will require discipline. Your habits of fast action may be difficult to control. But you will reap huge dividends if you quickly test for trivial versus important and apply the cyclical-diagnostic process to your important problems. Develop your sales team's problem-solving skills. Why not try it right now on (what seems to be) your toughest supervisory problem?

CHECKLIST

_____ Identify problems as unimportant or important by the test of: "could a decision hurt anyone; cost more than (your benchmark); and make a difference a year from now?".

_____ Do you make fast decisions on the unimportant and use a patient analytical process on the crucial decisions?

_____ Do you search for causes, identify key questions, consider consequences of solutions, and circle the problem several times before reaching a conclusion?

_____ Do you consult those involved or affected by the results of your decisions?

REFERENCE

1. This originated from "How to Think Straight," a process taught by the late Dr. William J. Reilly at 41 S.M.I. seminars I conducted with him from 1956 through 1963. After first visiting Japan in 1965, I altered the "scientific thought process" with some Japanese adaptations but still as a linear thought process. I saw 1,621 sales managers use the

process in seminars since then to solve their own toughest supervisory problems with good results. Reproduced below is the pocket card I developed summarizing that process. In 1987 I read the book *The Professional Decision-Thinker* by Ben Heirs (Dodd, Mead & Company, N.Y., 1986) which added great substance and suggested a cyclical process. I highly recommend reading Ben Heirs' book which explodes Western Myths about Decision Thinking.

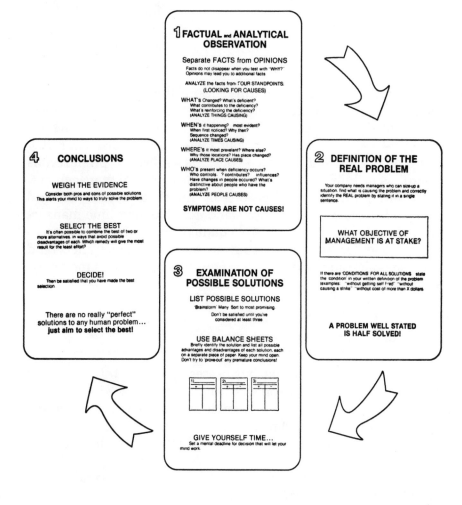

Chapter Five

How to Select and Recruit Better Sales Team Members

Let's turn now to the "Opportunity/Something Is Going Wrong" that is critical to the success or failure of most managers. The most important decision you ever make is whether or not to hire—or promote—a specific person to your sales staff. Mistakes in hiring and promotion will drag down your unit's sales and profit results regardless of how skilled you are in other areas of management. Make hiring/promotion decisions by hunch and you will find yourself lowering performance standards, blowing time management plans, and struggling to train untrainables and coach uncoachables. A bad decision in choosing one salesperson may affect (and infect) morale and performance of your other good staff members. Result: Turnover is bound to increase.

PICK STRONG PEOPLE

Strong people build strong businesses. Improve this cluster of your recruiting and selection skills and the result will be a drop in turnover. Just as a person is known by the company he or she keeps, your company is known by the people it keeps. Turnover is costly. It has but one cause: management failure. This management failure starts before the applicant is hired.

In the rest of this chapter, we suggest how sales managers can recruit and select better sales team members. Interviewing skills are briefly discussed. For more detail on how to find and qualify

FIGURE 5–1
An Opportunity/Something Is Going Wrong

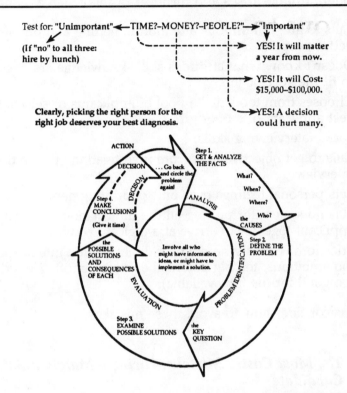

Test for: "Unimportant"◄—TIME?–MONEY?–PEOPLE?"—►"Important"

(If "no" to all three: hire by hunch)

YES! It will matter a year from now.

YES! It will Cost: $15,000–$100,000.

YES! A decision could hurt many.

Clearly, picking the right person for the right job deserves your best diagnosis.

ACTION

DECISION

Step 1.
GET & ANALYZE
THE FACTS

... Go back and circle the problem again!

What?

When?

Step 4.
MAKE
CONCLUSIONS

ANALYSIS

Where?

(Give it time)

the Who?
CAUSES

the
POSSIBLE
SOLUTIONS
AND
CONSEQUENCES
OF EACH

Involve all who might have information, ideas, or might have to implement a solution.

Step 2.
DEFINE THE
PROBLEM

EVALUATION

PROBLEM IDENTIFICATION

Step 3.
EXAMINE
POSSIBLE SOLUTIONS

the
KEY
QUESTION

sales representatives, read the NSSTE Sales Success Booklet by John H. Rose: *"How to Recruit, Interview, and Select Productive Sales Representatives,"* Tel. (800) 752–7613 or Fax (407) 323–3116.

Refer to the illustration of the Cyclical-Scientific Thought Process (Figure 4–1) and then test Recruiting and Selection for importance.

Because selection mistakes are so costly, it is clear that a manager must follow (clockwise and in order) the cyclical-scientific thought process through the four steps: 1. Analyze the facts (job specs and candidates' qualifications) subjectively and objectively for causes, 2. Identify the objective (what makes each candidate tick?), 3. Evaluate pros and cons of many possible (candidates) solutions, 4. Decide, while avoiding the counter-productive/counter-clockwise, snap decision.

Analyze Causes of Selection Failures

Most often, trouble arises and turnover results when a manager:

1. Fails to give continuous attention to getting and building better people.
2. Doesn't know what attitudes-skills-knowledge are needed to fit the specific job.
3. Chooses from too small a pool of applicants or selects the best applicant of a poor group.
4. Lacks interviewing skills.
5. Fails to get objective facts from investigation outside the interview.
6. Lets personal feelings overcome good judgment.
7. Has no system for putting all the information about the applicant together to arrive at a logical decision.
8. Tries to hire reps who are over-qualified (too intelligent, too ambitious, too big potential earners—in other words too good for the job available).

Let us consider how to avoid these mistakes.

The Most Costly Mistake: Hiring a Marginal Sales Candidate

Suppose you are confronted with an open territory and, in the absence of better candidates, you decide to hire the one person who comes along looking like he or she just *might* be able to do the job (mistake #3 . . . selecting the best applicant of a poor group). You should recognize that a mediocre salesperson—one who is just good enough to keep but not quite bad enough to discharge— is the costliest item on your company's payroll! Once hired, you will struggle with that person from appraisal to appraisal hoping the individual will get better and improve sales, while your entire district's efforts are pulled down. It would be far better to leave the territory open while expanding your search for candidates. If you are going to make a mistake in hiring, you might be better off making a big one by hiring a bum or by using contract, temporary sales labor. (The obvious misfit will be gone before the mistake gets too costly!) The best thing to do is keep on recruiting continuously even when you have no openings so you have a ready list of top quality candidates (corrects mistake #1).

A MAJOR PURCHASING DECISION

Recognize that your role in hiring is that of "buying" a service. You are purchasing one of the most costly commodities in the world. Costs vary by company but to hire and train a new sales representative costs between $15,000 and $100,000 in direct expenses during the first year. And that cost estimate does not include business lost by the inept salesperson. A common mistake (a combination of mistakes 4, 5, and 6 listed on page 44) made by sales managers is to try to sell recruits on coming to work for the company rather than paying full attention to being a discrete buyer of salespower. Inform candidates about what the job is but do not slip into your normal selling role. A smart buyer of a thing that may cost the company $100,000 (and, if not the right material, will be lost within a year) studies his/her purchasing needs, develops product specifications, and shops the best sources for the product fitting those specs; rather than buying impulsively.

The process and skills we suggest for choosing people for your staff resemble how the skilled physician builds a successful medical practice: Know your stuff. Attract a large following through word of mouth, reputation, and continual recruitment. Devote full attention with each recruit to be both subjective (in interviewing) and objective (in tests and examinations). Identify each candidate's key need and weigh all the pros and cons and probable reactions (based on past performance) of each treatment (candidate). Then, after verifying critical assumptions, make your diagnosis and employment offer. You should proceed like this:

1. Know what you are looking for.
2. Continually recruit.
3. Effectively use multiple screens: interviews and factual analysis.
4. Qualify and verify attitudes-skills-knowledge.

5. Evaluate top candidates.
6. Decide; make the offer.

"But I seldom have to hire anyone," you say, "besides, others in my company do that!"

Get involved in selecting your staff. What if the sales reps you supervise were hired by someone else? What if others do initial recruiting and hiring? If you "inherited" your sales force, find out all you can about each rep and build on their strengths. The technique shown earlier of evaluating possible solutions by writing down a balance sheet of pros and cons for each alternative might also help you evaluate staff, and candidates for your staff. In one column, list the person's strengths; in the other, list needs for development. Make sure that from now on you participate in decisions of who is hired to work under your supervision. Here's why. In the mind of the recruit, "the person who said 'OK, you're hired' is the person who can also 'fire'" . . . and that person is who the recruit will try most to please after hiring. Also, you take pride in your decisions. It is only natural. You will work harder through good management to prove your selection was the right choice. In making right people choices, the place to start is to clarify job demands.

KNOW WHAT YOU ARE LOOKING FOR

The first step in buying salespower is to know what you are looking for: the specific demands of the sales territory (job) that needs to be filled. Familiarize yourself with the sales job you need filled. Study the job description, or the list of prioritized Responsibilities, Indicators, and Goals (See Chapter 2.). The latter reminds one of what the job is and what it looks like when well done. But you must translate that into position (job) requirements (job specs)—that is, what the job requires of the applicant—so you can develop the representative specifications (people specs). In other words, to do these responsibilities to standard, what must an applicant bring to the job in order to perform properly? What kinds of attitudes, skills, and knowledge are common success factors of your most successful salespeople? One company (Airco Gas) studied its most successful sales representatives and identified these common success factors:

- Business/technical knowledge.
- Initiating.
- Planning, organizing, administering.
- Problem solving.
- Directing, controlling, facilitating.
- Communicating.
- Working with individuals and groups.
- Staffing and employee development (if job leads to management of others).

A veteran sales manager of construction equipment said: "The sales reps I hired who were most successful were ones who really knew the customers' businesses and product knowledge; overcame the lack of advanced college degrees with hard work; planned and organized well; and knew how to solve problems for and with their customers."

What are the characteristics you look for in each applicant for a position on your sales staff?

A worksheet can be a big help in organizing your list of sales rep success factors. Once you have a clear list of these requirements, you can prepare a listing of the best bonafide occupational questions to ask of each candidate to explore what the candidate would bring to the job. Figure 5-2 is a very simple worksheet you can use for preparing to effectively recruit and interview sales reps. It will help you identify the attitudes, skills, and knowledge you are looking for in this specific job.

Another way of listing representatives specifications is to group specs for Minimum Education, Selling Experience, Job Stability, Achievements, Interests, Driving Record, Appearance, Manner, Personality, Communication Skills, Mental Alertness, and Knowledge. With an organized list of specs, you can develop key questions to ask to uncover how the candidate meets each spec. A sample is shown in Figure 5-3. It is used by a consumer products company.

FIGURE 5–2
Position Requirements Worksheet

Instructions: 1. Determine list of job responsibilities for position. 2. Prioritize responsibilities in order of importance to job performance. 3. Identify attitude, skills, and knowledge and other requirements needed to perform job. 4. Prepare questions for interview.

Job Responsibilities	Attitude, Skills, Knowledge, Other	Bonafide Occupational Questions

FIGURE 5–3

Representative Specifications	*Ask and Probe about . . .*

1. *Education:*

How achieved.	"When and why?" "Graduate?" "How paid for?"
Major.	"How was major decided?" "Why chosen?"
Courses.	"What value?" "Which courses useful?" "Likes/dislikes?" "Which most difficult?"
Grades.	"What grades?" "What best at?" "Why?"
Instructors.	"Describe your best teacher." "Worst/why?"
Time. Extracurricular.	"What else done, and how got involved?"
Feelings (responsibility).	"How do you feel about your education?"

Min.: Four year college graduate or equivalent.

"Knock outs": Unreasonable changes of major. Excessive time acquiring a degree with invalid reasons.

- -

2. *Work experience:*

Selling usually not required, but desirable. Progression of work experience, follow through and success in past. Provide evidence.	"Tell me about work record . . . background?" "Sales jobs . . . similarities?" "What like most in that job?" "Why?" "What dislike?" "Why?" "How handled?" "What did you learn?" "How long did it last?" "Why leave?" "What done next?" *Knock-outs:* Never tried or repeated failures. Disagreements with bosses or co-workers, patterns of undesirable behavior.

- -

3. *Job Stability:*

More than two full-time positions in last five years is a caution sign which must be carefully evaluated.	"What did you do when you left the . . . job?" "How long?" "Why change?" "What then?" (Repeat work questions.) *Knock-outs:* Three or more full-time jobs in five years without very valid, convincing reasons.

- -

FIGURE 5–3 (concluded)

4. *Achievements:*
    Accomplishments in past on and off jobs, educat., under difficult conditions. Worked hard. Supported self and others. Shows desire to always learn more. Finished what started.

    "What one thing are you most proud of?" "How support self and others?" "Extra-curricular activities?" "Biggest challenges?" "What are your strengths?" "Weaknesses?" "Why should I hire you?"

    Knock-outs: Record of quit, quit, quit. Low G.P.A. (grade point average) without other commitments. Evidence of "professional student" or obviously overqualified. Past goals seldom achieved.

5. *Interest:*
    Keen interest in selling, expressed in your business. Some leisure time activities that contribute to both mental and physical well-being.

    "What kind of work do you want to do?" "What brought you to pick this company?" "What do you know about us?" "What do you think an actual day working for us would be like?" "Why should we hire you?"

    Knock-outs: Obvious inability to learn. Too far out of consumer products sales. Over-qualified with no opportunity.

6. *Driving Record:*
    Valid license. Safe driving record. No revocations, no DUI.

    "Do you have a valid license?" "Any DUIs?" "What experience driving do you have?"

    Knock-outs: Revoked or no license.

CONTINUALLY RECRUIT

Avoid crash recruiting programs to locate a candidate for a vacant territory. Here's how: Continuously recruit even when all assignments are filled. Ask about who are the top salespeople in the area. Write down contact phone numbers of top prospects suggested to you. When you hire one finalist from several qualified candidates, keep the records of the other qualifieds not hired so you can contact them if another sales position becomes available. This "ready" file and continuous recruiting develops a reserve of qualified candidates, some of whom may be currently employed and willing to wait until an opening occurs.

Sources of Candidates

Know where to look. There are no revolutionary new avenues to successful recruitment, but past experience of many managers has shown the following to be effective sources for recruiting sales representatives. These sources are listed here in order of preference based on past results, but may not necessarily apply in your situation. The point is to use sources that provide quality with quantity. Sources are: referrals from employees, personal acquaintances, business contacts, and professors or teachers of Sales and Marketing; direct applicant contact; employment agencies; newspaper ads; and college and university placement bureaus.

Referrals from employees. Referrals from employees are your best source of good applicants. Especially from your own sales representatives. Encourage your reps to recommend prospective employees. Some companies pay a finder's fee for referring sales applicants who are subsequently hired. If the fee is payable after the new hire proves satisfactory (is on the payroll a certain period of time), you tie two people to the company: the new sales rep and sponsoring employee.

Personal acquaintances. Let your friends and other personal acquaintances know you are always on the lookout for outstanding sales applicants. Give them a brief summary of your specifications and an equally brief description of the job and its opportunities. They may be able to put you into contact with a top sales candidate for immediate or future employment.

Business contacts. Tell your business contacts of your desire for top sales applicants in your regular contacts.

If you are in an area of a military facility, see if they have a full- or part-time Separations Officer or Personnel Officer who may be able to direct you to high caliber, well-qualified people.

Customers are potential recruiting sources. Many employ college students on a part-time basis and do not expect to hold them beyond graduation. Recruiting at this level often offers you an opportunity to observe the work habits and attitudes of the prospective applicant in an actual working situation. Do this only with the permission and cooperation of the customer so your efforts are not taken as personnel raiding or piracy.

Sales and Marketing professors. If your company seeks college-trained sales representatives (for technology or sales and marketing reasons), cultivate targeted professors at schools in your area. This pays huge dividends in pre-screened referrals. Referrals by Sales and Marketing professors are used effectively by at least one company in what it calls a "Pre-Recruiting Program." Sales managers follow a program aimed at increasing the number of highly qualified sales-interested graduates seeking sales careers with the company. As a result, college professors give the company's local management a list of the top candidates about to graduate. The district manager follows these steps:

I. Target one area recruiting school.

II. Cultivate influential campus contacts by offering to bring real-world sales and marketing experience into classes.

III. Make recruiting material available through the Career Services Department.

IV. Carry out Pre-Recruiting functions by participation in marketing class presentations, Job Fairs, Business Club presentations, and Professor-Department Chair meetings.

(These first four are performed on a continuous basis without regard to the level of recruitment.)

V. Identify high potential sales candidates through interested students, professor recommendations, and pre-screening of resumes.

VI. Establish interview date.

VII. Open House conducted at on-campus location with display of company products, recruiting materials in informal gathering of invited interviewees.

VIII. Conduct scheduled interviews.

IX. Feedback. Update campus contacts on recruiting results.

Your skills (sharpened by rehearsals) are key to implementing such a program. At Dial Corp., field sales managers in training for "Visiting Professorships" devote a week of selection skill practice that includes conducting classes at a university.

Direct applicant contact.   When applicants come to you, they may be showing more initiative or interest in your company than is present in someone contacted through newspaper ads, placement bureaus, or employment agencies. The direct contact applicant who answers your screening questions favorably and meets your requirements may well turn out to be an above-average prospect for employment.

Employment agencies.   A good employment agency is an excellent source of qualified applicants. The agency can save you time. Its function is to collect, screen, and refer qualified applicants according to your specifications. However, it is a rather expensive source since the average cost per applicant hired is approximately 17 percent of the first year's salary. If you use agencies, pick one or two good agencies in various parts of your district and work closely with this limited number. Supply a complete job description and give them a thorough understanding of your sales representative specifications. Build a close personal relationship with the agency staff so they refer the agency's best prospects to you. Advise the agency that your company is an Equal Opportunity Employer, if it is. Have a clear understanding of their fees. If your company pays all or part of the agency's fee, let them know your policy. IMPORTANT! Tell the agency up front that you will not tolerate them sending you mediocre applicants. When an employment agency routinely sends obviously unqualified applicants, sever the relationship and utilize another agency.

Newspaper ads. Use this recruiting source in conjunction with other sources or when other sources fail. The use of newspaper ads has the following *advantages:* reaches many candidates in a short period of time; produces a large pool of qualified candidates; and, is relatively inexpensive—no fees have to be paid. The *disadvantages:* not all candidates who respond are qualified; increased management time is required to screen the applicants prior to setting up interviews. The number may be overwhelming.

College and university placement bureaus. Some schools maintain separate offices to serve graduating students and alumni. If you are to enjoy a productive relationship with these placement bureaus, familiarize the director and staff with your standards and requirements. Help them understand your sales representative's job and the advantages and opportunities available to graduates. Sell them and a few professors and you multiply the effectiveness of recruiting efforts. This relationship can be established through short but frequent calls when you are working in the area with one of your representatives. Once graduates have been hired and are successful, they will be helpful in recruiting future candidates from their alma mater.

USE MULTIPLE SCREENS EFFECTIVELY

Determining a job applicant's attitude (as well as many other things) requires personal interviewing. But, too often, the decision to hire is based on what the interviewer likes or dislikes in an individual and not on "what is the job?" and "can this applicant do it?"

To make the determination that an applicant can and will do this job (and not waste your time), you must screen out unqualified applicants and screen in the fully qualified applicants. The successful sales candidate must pass through many screens: (1) your study of the résumé or job inquiry letter; (2) the screening interview; (3) your study of the application form; (4) the selection interview; (5) your check of work references, transcripts, and verification of information; (6) work exposure (ride with a current sales rep); and (7) your decision to offer the job.

What to Look For

The best indication of what a person will do in the future is accurate information on what he or she has done in the past. Every individual is a unique product of the attitudes, skills, and knowledge accumulated all through life. Especially important for you to know is the person's reactions developed during their formative years and education, during their work experience and present life, and how those demonstrated reactions relate to the job requirements. You must dig skillfully with all seven tools (screens). You know—from having reviewed the specs—the kinds of attitudes, skills, and knowledge the new recruit will have to bring to the job (or quickly grow into) in order to sell successfully in the territory assigned. Putting the applicants through many screens enables you to select the best. Because job applicants may talk up their good points and hide the bad, you need to dig deeper with more than a single, simple interview. Very few diamonds are found on the surface!

Let's look at the seven screens in more detail.

Screen 1: Scan the résumé or letter of application. See if the inquirer meets enough of the job requirements to warrant scheduling a screening interview. All applicants—whether qualified or not—should be treated in a friendly, polite and fair manner.

Screen 2: The screening interview. This enables you to immediately eliminate the obviously unqualified and make arrangements for those qualified to receive an application and to set up a mutually convenient time for the selection interview. It can be done either by phone or in person. If there is a choice, the applicant should be seen in person because this offers the added advantage of being able to see how the applicant looks, acts, and talks. The ability to sell oneself in the interview is a clue to the applicant's ability to sell your products.

Make the screening interview brief. Your questions are simple and direct on the key job requirements so you can quickly screen out unqualified applicants. Use questions like:

Did you graduate from college? (if required for sales).

What was your major?

What kind of position are you seeking?

What work experience have you had?

What were the dates of your last employment?

What type of work did you do?

What minimum salary would you accept?

Are you willing to relocate?

Are you willing to travel overnight if necessary?

Do you have a valid driver's license?

What brought you to apply? What do you know about our company?

Don't take time to go into the job description. Whenever it is obvious that the applicant's answer indicates the lack of the basic job requirements, politely but firmly terminate the interview.

When the screening interview is complete and it is apparent that the applicant has the basic requirements, briefly describe the job. If the applicant is interested in pursuing the job further, offer an application. If accepted, set up a reasonable time for the applicant to complete and return the application. *Important:* Your application form should be given only to those applicants who meet your basic job requirements as determined by the screening interview. But, any applicant—whether qualified or not—who insists on receiving an application should be given one.

Screen 3: The application form. This is designed to: (1) Provide basic information on the applicant's background; (2) Assist you in planning the selection interview; (3) Indicate areas of the applicant's background requiring more explanation or clarification; and (4) Provide a permanent record of the applicant that will become a permanent part of his/her personnel folder.

In addition to the application, you may want the applicant to complete a list of his or her home addresses in a chronological order for the past 5–10 years. This information is useful for background checks.

Review the application form carefully. Allow ample time for doing this between receipt and the time set for the second (selection) interview. When reviewing the application, look for: Completeness—has every question been answered? (If not applicable fill in with "N/A".) Has it been signed and dated? (You must get it signed before background checks are made.) Are the answers vague? (Statements such as "lack of opportunity" or "better pay" need further clarification.) Exaggeration of past accomplishments? Numerous job changes? Unusual salary requirements? Difficulty with previous employers? Travel or relocation restrictions? Inconsistencies or incomplete dates of schooling and employment?

Screen 4: The selection interview. This second or selection interview provides you with an opportunity to obtain facts and information from the applicant, relevant to employment, that is unavailable from other sources, and evaluate qualifications against the attitudes, skills, and knowledge required for the job. It also provides, to the applicant, job and company information in order that the applicant has a factual basis for accepting or rejecting employment if offered. By its conclusion, you can decide, on the basis of the information obtained from the interview, whether the applicant should be rejected, recommended for employment (contingent on verification of information given), or scheduled for further interviewing.

No one can size up people simply by looking at them or talking with them in generalities. To get the information needed to properly measure and evaluate an applicant, use effective interviewing techniques: prepare, establish rapport, draw out information, give information, close, evaluate, and recommend.

When conducting the selection interview, make sure you stay within the guidelines of the Equal Employment Opportunities laws. Only ask questions that are job related. Let's assume you've done thorough preparation, received the applicant into a comfortable, private place, established rapport, and explained why you have a job opening.

In order to get information, you must listen and observe. The best questions won't get you very far if you don't listen carefully and observe fully. It is not easy to listen actively, evaluate, keep control of the interview, and plan the next question at the same time. (See Chapter 9 for an understanding of all the tools of questioning and listening.) Be sure that you are really hearing all that the candidate is saying; concentrate. Listen with empathy. Be interested, attentive, understanding, and nonjudgmental. When candidates sense disapproval, they temper or change their answers as a reaction to your expression. You will get the applicant to open up and tell so much more by you reflecting a neutral attitude of: "It's OK, tell me more . . . , um humm, I see, what else? . . . how do you feel about it?"; and adding comments like: "Sometimes we might wish we could do things over, if you could, what would you do differently?"

Record job related information uncovered during the interview. Writing it down helps you make a thorough evaluation later, and also helps you compare candidates. Record answers as they are given. Most candidates won't mind your taking notes; however, you may want to mention that you will be taking notes before you start writing. Put down key words spoken by the candidate; not your judgmental or snap interpretation. Your interview notes are an important selection tool, and as such they must be clear, concise, and accurate.

Structure your line of questions by "funnelling." Funnelling is an interviewing technique for organizing, controlling, and analyzing interview information flow. It works by determining major categories to explore; within each category move from general, broad questions to specific, detailed questions. Your specific, detailed questions can be based on indicators picked up from answers to your general questions. Figure 5–4 explains this process.

Avoid "yes-or-no" questions. Use short answer questions only for confirmation; not information getting.

As the interviewee produces information in response to your questioning and encouragement, keep your yardstick in mind—behavior that is characteristic of the attitudes, skills, and knowledge needed to perform responsibilities and tasks associated with the job. During the interview you should form a hypothesis about how the person would act in a selling situation and ask questions to test your hypothesis. Listen for little things said and those things not said. A particular adjective to describe a previous supervisor may lead to the revelation of a negative attitude toward the boss. This should be probed. Here are other caution signs:

1. Record of failure. If a review of the applicant's education, previous jobs, or military indicate failure or even a lack of success, it can be expected he/she may fail again. (You are searching for people who achieve, finish what they start, have a history of succeeding from early life right up to now.) If the interviewee has

FIGURE 5–4
The Funnelling Process

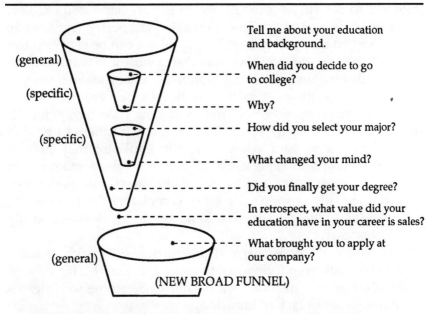

(general)   Tell me about your education
                            and background.

(specific)   When did you decide to go
                            to college?

                            Why?

(specific)   How did you select your major?

                            What changed your mind?

                            Did you finally get your degree?

                            In retrospect, what value did your
                            education have in your career is sales?

(general)   What brought you to apply at
                            our company?

(NEW BROAD FUNNEL)

failed to sell anything in the past and is not selling you now (not being persistent in seeking the job), he/she will probably fail again in the sales job.

2. Variety of jobs. If the applicant has changed jobs often—even though claiming these were to better him/herself—it generally denotes restlessness, which might be costly to the company if this person is hired. Also, check the time pattern of the job history. There might be an indication as to how long the applicant might be expected to stay in the job.

3. Extreme salary change. A sharp reduction in income from previous employment is a danger sign. If this is severe enough to cause a change in the applicant's standard of living, in many cases they will not stay.

4. Recent business failure. If the applicant recently disposed of a personal business venture, carefully review with him or her the reason and the applicant's desire to work for you. Quite often such a person is seeking a temporary respite or an opportunity to recuperate financially and will have a strong desire to get back in their own business.

5. Unusual intellectual achievement. If the applicant has advanced degrees or unusual academic achievements, this must be evaluated to determine if the applicant is truly interested in sales. Frequently this type of applicant is seeking temporary work, while looking for better opportunities. This applicant can be very effective in sales, however, and may have potential to move into management.

6. Family business. A special caution should be taken if there is a family-owned business in the applicant's background. Check closely. If there is, question the applicant thoroughly for an indication of his or her feeling about it. If the business or type of work is related to your company's, the applicant may just be seeking training and experience. Chances are the applicant will say she/he wants no part of the family business, but our experience in resignations shows a pattern completely the reverse. Do not consider a family business a knockout in all cases. Carefully review this area.

What you look for is that difficult to define "spark" or drive within that pushes an individual to accomplishment. This drive is so important that it may cause a person to overcome weaknesses in other abilities or lack of knowledge: one reason why determining past performance—the track record—of each applicant is your best predictor of future performance.

Answer the applicant's questions honestly and clearly, but hold your enthusiasm for the job and the company in check until you are sure the applicant is adequately qualified. Many inexperienced interviewers frequently fall into the trap of overselling the job in the beginning of the interview. This is because they act on their personal impressions and intuition. As the interview progresses and the applicant is found to be unsuited, the task of rejection becomes more difficult and unpleasant for both the interviewer and the applicant.

Too often, good applicants are lost to competitors because they did not have a clear understanding of the advantages of working for your company. Tell them about the job:

1. Territory. The work schedule and how it is organized. Time required for planning, travel, and reporting. Nature of products and their position in the market. Type of customers and how contacted. General responsibilities. Compensation plan. Nature and extent of supervision. Advancement opportunities.

2. Training provided. This is a very important factor for representatives who are unfamiliar with your business. Initial training. Continuous training. Development programs. Sales meetings. Tell them about the company.

3. History. Size, sales, and growth (Annual Report). Research expenditures. Management structure. The need for future managers. Promotion policy. Personal and organization growth. Expenses and transportation. Insurance and retirement programs. Vacation policy. Esprit de corps. Stock purchase. Credit Union. Employee Savings Plan.

Make sure the applicant wants the job. "I didn't know I'd have to spend so much time in an auto" (or some other statement of surprise) accompanies too many newly hired sales reps' announcements of quitting after only a few days or a month on the job. Representatives who quickly resign probably would not have accepted employment if they had been given the opportunity to better comprehend the many aspects of a representative's job. You can avoid this. Ask the candidate to ride with an experienced representative. A day in the field with a good, experienced representative will help answer many of the questions an applicant may have about the job. Brief the experienced sales representative on exactly what is expected to be accomplished during a full day's work with a variety of calls. The ride with allows an out of the office screen by a designated sales representative.

Even though you cannot make a definite job offer at this time, the favorable applicant should leave the interview encouraged and enthusiastic about the prospects of becoming a sales rep for your company. Schedule the ride with an experienced rep (phone numbers, and so on). Tell this applicant when he/she should expect to hear from you. Give a specific length of time.

The Interviewer's Grid (Figure 5-5) is a score sheet for the interviewer's use *immediately* postinterview. Its purpose is to summarize application and interview information on how well the applicant stacks up on the basic job requirements. You are advised to tailor the rating form to fit the most important requirements specifically for a sales representative in your industry and company. For more detailed forms and a summary sheet for desired behavioral characteristics, see NSSTE's Sales Success Booklet "How to Recruit, Interview, and Select Productive Sales Representatives."

FIGURE 5–5
Interviewer's Grid

Applic. Name _____ Date _____ Interviewer _____

REPRESENTATIVE SPECIFICATIONS	FORMATIVE YRS & EDUCATION + + + 0 - =	PRESENT LIFE & WORK EXPERIENCE + + + 0 - =	RATING + + + 0 - =
BUSINESS/ TECHNICAL KNOWLEDGE			
INITIATIVE			
PLANNING, ORGANIZING, ADMINISTRATION			
PROBLEM SOLVING			
DIRECTING, CONTROLLING, FACILITATING			
COMMUNI-CATING			
WORK W/ INDIVIDUALS and GROUPS			
STAFFING and EMPLOYEE DEVELOPMENT (if appl.)			

QUALIFY AND VERIFY

As pointed out earlier, matching the right person to the job is one of the most important decisions you make as a manager. In your evaluation at the conclusion of the selection (second) interview, think through these points:

• How would I predict this applicant's future success in the sales job? Do I have information to support my thesis?

- Did I look beyond any stereotypes I might have in order to be sure personality traits fit the job?
- Is the education suitable? Does it relate to the job requirements? What other education related factors are relevant?
- Is the experience relevant? Can she/he sell? Does the applicant's work history show potential for growth?
- How does this applicant compare with other applicants? What are the positive factors and negative factors? Have I eliminated all personal biases from consideration?

Screen 5: Check work references and verify information. The checking of references is the second most important step in the selection process—the careful and complete selection interview being the most significant selection tool. This step consists of verifying the statements made on the application form. Most job application forms contain a statement like this: "I authorize persons, schools, current employer (if applicable), and previous employers and organizations named in this application (and accompanying résumé, if any) to provide the company with any relevant information that may be required to arrive at an employment decision." Following the completion and signing of an application by a job applicant, reference checks may be made.

Why should you check references? Applicants will slant their stories in their own favor, and some will cover up and exaggerate. Because of this, it is essential that their histories be checked with other sources to obtain complete and accurate facts and verify.

Previous employers are your best source of information about the applicant. Contact the immediate supervisor whenever possible. Immediate supervisors know from first hand experience how well the applicant did the job. They have observed the applicant in action and seen him or her work under pressure. Frequently they may know of some personal weakness, or strength, which may affect job performance. Checking previous employers is usually done by telephone. To get the best results from the telephone check, call the last two or three employers, but do not contact a present employer until you have the applicant's permission. If possible, talk to the immediate supervisor. Identify yourself, your position, and your company and state your reason for calling: to verify information. Properly approached, a supervisor will frequently be willing to discuss a previous employee's record. Don't be discouraged by the refusal of some references to provide any information other than dates of employment. Other references will be more cooperative.

Carefully listen to how things are said. Most people reveal true feelings and opinions in their manner, their tone of voice, hesitations, and the inflections just as much or more than they do in the words they use.

Make long distance calls if necessary. The cost of telephone calls is inexpensive compared to hiring the wrong person.

Information received through reference checks is strictly confidential. Under no circumstances should you reveal to the applicant or to other persons anything a previous employer has disclosed.

Screen 6: Expose the applicant to a sample of work.   The day in the field in a ride with one of your experienced sales reps allows your rep to see how the applicant reacts in sales situations. Following a day with the applicant, require your sales representative to provide you with a playback on what happened (through discussion and a summarizing letter). Ask your rep his/her opinion of the applicant. Does the rep think that the applicant would pull his/her share of district sales? Does he/she want the applicant on the team? (The letter will become part of the applicant's file.) This practice will help you obtain additional information about the applicant. It also tells your representative that you value his or her opinion.

Also, have the applicant contact you at the conclusion of the day in the field. This affords you both the opportunity to ask questions and obtain information relative to the mutual decision on employment. (You will be deciding whether or not you will recommend the applicant for employment. The applicant will be deciding if she/he should accept the job, if offered.)

EVALUATE TOP CANDIDATES AND DECIDE

Screen 7: Weigh and decide which candidate to offer the job.   To this point you have fed your mind with information on a number of qualified candidates. Don't become careless and comfortable in your hunches and prejudices. Everyone has strengths and weaknesses, plusses and minuses. Always demand from yourself supporting evidence for your judgments. (A quick review of the problem-solving techniques in Chapter 4 would suggest you prepare a balance sheet for each of your leading candidates for the job.) Compare all your accumulated data: the "Interviewer's Grids," application forms, notes on reference checks, and reports from your reps' ride withs.

Your future, and the future success of your sales organization, is determined by how skillfully you recruit, select, train, coach, manage, and develop your sales team. Finding and selecting the right person for the right job makes subsequent training, field direction, and supervision effective. The right person is one whose qualifications indicate they can do the job and will do the job. Make your decision. Make the offer and sell the person on accepting it. Then be satisfied that you have selected the best material with which to build your team.

Never give reasons for rejection. You may screen or interview and subsequently reject many applicants before anyone is hired. Regardless of what your reasons are for rejecting an applicant, they should never be conveyed to that individual. Doing so is a serious mistake, and in some cases could go so far as to create legal complications.

Even though the basis of rejection appears obvious to you, this may not be clear or even acceptable to the applicant. More often than not, your seemingly good intentions will be met by a counter argument which creates problems rather than solutions. This not only wastes time, but frequently causes resentment and hostility in the rejected applicant.

Avoid discussions of this nature by telling interviewed applicants they will be advised of your decision after you have completed your scheduled interviews with other qualified applicants. It is good business practice to advise the unsuccessful applicants by letter of your decision. Do not get trapped into discussing your reasons for not selecting an applicant. Tell him or her that in your opinion you selected a better qualified applicant.

A manager must stay within the law and make selections for employment without regard to race, color, creed, national origin, age, sex, marital status, or disability. *Remember:* Employment shall be on the basis of merit, qualifications, and competency. As a sales manager, that is what you want in each new team member: the best qualified to do the job in terms of job-related behavioral characteristics; one who can do and will do the job.

CHECKLIST

_____ Do you have a ready file of qualified candidates on hand at all times in the event you do have a job opening?

_____ Have you determined what specific attitudes, skills, and knowledge you look for in applicants for sales representative?

_____ Do you pick from a large enough pool of applicants to assure getting the best?

_____ Are you ever alert during selection to prevent personal feelings from overcoming good judgment?

_____ Do you use all the screens available to you in selecting?

_____ Have you made a conscious effort to improve your interviewing skills during the past six months?

Chapter Six

How to Teach Your Team

A sales manager asks: "How can I accelerate the growth of my people?" That's an important question to consider because upper management is measuring you by your staff's growth. Your boss looks at things like: How many of your sales representatives are meeting or exceeding sales quota and production goals; how many are currently promotable; to what extent; are all your reps competent in their current jobs; how much growth are they showing since you took over the district; how's morale; is turnover under control?

As manager, you are responsible for training your sales staff. You bear primary accountability for their effectiveness. That includes their attitudes, skills, and knowledge, three abilities that you affect more than anyone, other than the salespeople themselves.

CRITICAL SKILLS FOR MANAGERS

The most important skill needed by a front line sales manager is the skill of teaching others. Yet many managers have never had formal training in how to instruct. Not knowing how to train, some managers rely on sink or swim by simply throwing the salesperson out into the territory; others use the watch me swim technique by doing all the selling themselves so the would be student never gets in the water until after the instructor has left. Either approach causes drowning—in the pool or in the market. Training sales representatives to become more effective is essential to both the rep's and manager's success.

Here, from experience, are ten tips managers should follow in training their sales staff:

1. Manage while developing people. Get the business today while building people to grow your company's business in the future! Sales Reps are energy packages. Your job is to get a higher and sustained application of that energy.

2. A manager can go as far, and accomplish as much, as he or she wants to so long as the manager is not particularly obsessed with taking credit. Be sure to give credit to your staff; you will gain better results.

3. Training is not something you do *to* another person. But you can and must help them learn. We all learn through discovery: your best teaching is to arrange for your learners to discover. Likewise, you don't motivate others; you can only help them to motivate themselves.

4. Training is more effective with those who wish to be trained! Remember this when recruiting and selecting staff.

5. Telling is not training! People learn by *doing*. Training that does not include active participation is wasted time. Take the learner through all four steps of good instruction: preparation of the learner; presentation of the skill; performing (with coaching); and follow up.

6. Most development is on the job. For a person to develop, they need to know what is expected; the opportunity to perform; to know how they're doing; assistance when and as needed; and to be rewarded on results! Another way of stating these is to say that climate, feedback, input, and output are the key factors of performance and growth. Both formal (periodic) coaching and informal (day-to-day) coaching are required to do this.

7. Take advantage of training aids and personally follow through on any company (or outside) training provided your people! The role of the training department is that of a catalyst for business and people development. You are responsible for seeing that your reps develop.

8. Field sales managers are the best trainers. They must be trained first and foremost in how to train!

9. A manager must help his or her salespeople to be able to manage their own territories and allow them to use their talents! Be a positive pygmalion; your faith in their ability

FIGURE 6-1

From Rubik's Cube

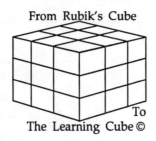

To
The Learning Cube ©

and in your own abilities as mentor will cause growth to happen.

10. Be most concerned with what is right, not who is right!

Before we look at how to train, another question needs to be answered: "How does the learner learn?". This is important because our natural tendency in attempting to teach needs discipline. Just like our mind jumps when faced with a problem, our sales experience makes us jump in and pile details on the new sales recruit with too much, too soon. A sales manager often knows the sales job too well—and overlooks the tricky points that stump the beginner (who is unfamiliar with the sales job).

HOW DO SALES REPS LEARN?

We learn by discovery, by doing, bit by bit, building block by building block, attaching something new—attitude, skill, and knowledge—to something we already know how to do.

The Learning Cube© [1]

Do you remember Rubik's Cube? At one time this puzzle—a cube made up of many smaller, multicolored blocks—was the hottest item in the toy business.

A lifetime of learning is like assembling those six-sided, multicolored blocks (see Figure 6-1). Kids everywhere were fidgeting with the three dimensional Rubik's Cube of smaller multicolored

FIGURE 6–2
The Learning Cube

FIGURE 6–3
The Job Requirements 'Hole'

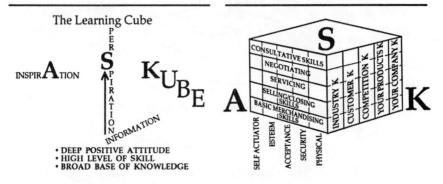

blocks, twisting and turning the little ones to match up the colors to each of the six big sides. The concept of a three dimensional Learning Cube clarifies the learning process and has great relevance and usefulness in:

- Job analysis.
- Job definition.
- Recruiting.
- Candidate selection.
- Training.

- Development.
- Staffing.
- Career decisions.
- Management development.
- Training of trainers.

Our learning also involves twisting and turning small three-dimensional bits, or blocks, of intelligence until we can hook each to something we already know. Like Rubik's Cube, the Learning Cube has three dimensions. You will instantly recognize them: "Attitude," "Skill," and "Knowledge." Every piece of know-how involves all three—attitude, skill, and knowledge—and nothing is truly learned until we are able to "stick" that new block to our bigger, accumulated, Learning Cube.

This "need to stick" points out the importance of performance and attitude in learning. We might think of learning as *inspiration* and *information* held together by *perspiration*. Few people make it as champion golfers or swimmers or sales representatives without heavy use of all three factors. Learning to do takes effort (attitude); perspiration (doing) makes knowledge stick. You may have noticed in Figure 6–2, we put *skill* on the vertical dimension because

FIGURE 6-4   **FIGURE 6-5**

BUILDING THE LEARNER'S

$$ASK_{U_{B_E}}$$

THRU SIX LEVELS

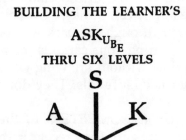

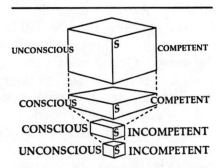

we want a high level of it. We added *knowledge* on the horizontal, symbolizing the desired broad base. We show depth as *attitude*. Voilà! The Learning Cube© or "ASKcube" is born.

In Figure 6-3 we show degrees (levels) by borrowing from motivation theory (Maslow's needs), specific selling skills, and classifications of knowledge.

Unlike Rubik's Cube, the Learning Cube grows—gets bigger as attitudes, skills, and knowledge increase. We add blocks of new learning.

You can use this model to list specific Job Requirements in terms of Attitudes, Skills, and Knowledge desired for a sales representative in your district. Then compare that need with how big a *cube* the learner brings to the job. The gap in each dimension is the rep's training need.

LEVELS OF COMPETENCY

A learner's cube grows in a different dimension as the learner moves up through each level of competency. For many years, trainers have referred to a "competency model" that consists of four levels. However, considering the learner's cube for a person moving through a career in the sales organization, we see that we must be concerned with at least six levels of competency (see Figure 6-4). It is important that you recognize the level of competency your trainee is on so you can most effectively and efficiently help them build to the next level.

Figure 6-5 shows that the lowest level of competency is the UNCONSCIOUS INCOMPETENT . . . the person who doesn't even realize he/she doesn't know something! In learning to drive an automobile, for example, the seven-year-old unconscious incompetent seeing the keys left in the family car, thinks: "Oh boy, I can drive!" and promptly puts the car through the back wall of the garage. Or the sales recruit who, during your campus interview, insists he/she can sell your product without knowing what it is, how it is used, or what customer need it fulfills. They don't know that they don't know!

At the second level of CONSCIOUS INCOMPETENCE, the incompetent sees that he/she has a training gap. They recognize a need to learn, and want to perform better. For example, the sales rep who calls you to find out how to do a new task or how she might approach a customer you formerly sold. In our driving example, the fifteen-year-old conscious incompetent realizes that he/she doesn't know how to drive and wants to learn badly enough that he/she starts watching others drive, finds out about cars, reads the Rules of the Road book, and pressures his or her parents into letting him or her enroll in driver's education courses. Note in Figure 6–5 how the "A" (attitude) side of the Learning ASKcube elongates at the CONSCIOUS INCOMPETENT level.

Most new sales recruits are at this level. They are green but really anxious to learn. Often, they function as sponges, soaking up all the information about their new sales job they can get. They may know the theory. But they are still unable to do the job right because they have not learned it in-the-muscles.

So you give training. If your instruction is good, it does not take long for the person (who wants to learn) to copy your motions and begin performing the task. If you emphasize why and coach students' performances, they become consciously competent. For example, while teaching a rep to close, you show and explain how to summarize the benefits that the customer has accepted and ask for a commitment. On the next several calls the sales rep does this, haltingly and deliberately, closing each time. You congratulate the rep on achieving competency. In teaching your child to drive, at about age 16 or 17 the CONSCIOUS COMPETENT, or third level of competency, arrives. In driver's education practice, the learner can back the car around the test barriers into a parallel parked position, knows and practices the rules of the road, but has to concentrate each step of the way, methodically, slowly, but correctly, while building skill.

Your sales trainee may be like this; able to make presentations, follow proper call procedures (just as you've taught), close a fair share of sales; but the trainee has to stay focused and concentrate on the task at hand. You've got a competent, steady performer who "goes by the book."

With repetition and practice, the task can be done habitually. Habits become honed skills. Soon, the performer moves to the level of unconscious competence. Within months of your teenager getting his/her own car (in the driving example), the learner becomes an UNCONSCIOUS COMPETENT. You know it when you hear rubber "burning" on the driveway as your teen leaves for school, covers the three miles to the school parking lot in three minutes, and could not tell you what route he/she took to get there! It was automatic.

Just like your senior sales rep who has been out there running the territory so long on automatic—no thinking—just winging it, call after call, day after day. This veteran knows the sales job so well he or she has no need for paper, doesn't need to review call procedure, or refer to call plans or price lists. The veteran rep has built such a rapport with his or her buyers that she/he may coast through calls on friendship, take shortcuts, and forget why some steps of a productive call have to be made. He or she is unconsciously competent.

Sales reps are efficient at this level of unconscious competency (if they don't forget; or if prices, products, or customers never change. Fortunately they do, and the newness prevents boredom and plateauing). Smart managers keep senior sales reps growing by giving new tasks, challenges, and telling them why. And by teaching them about changes in the marketplace.

Like you, the super sales rep's learning cube is, of course, much larger than the learning cubes of novice salespeople. When a manager's position in the company opens, it is usually the super sales rep who is promoted. But all that know-how, all that experience, knowledge, and sales skills acquired as a super performer is of no use as a manager unless the manager quickly acquires the new skills of mentorship and becomes a skilled trainer of salespeople. The typical super sales rep moved up to district sales manager is now at level five: unconscious incompetence as a mentor (see Figure 6-6). Overnight, the company created a new problem: It has lost its best sales producer and

FIGURE 6–6

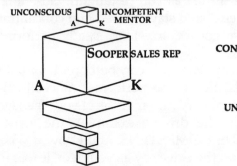

FIGURE 6–7

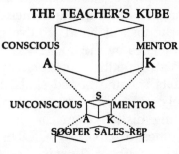

gained an incompetent manager. This ability to teach—to transfer to others what you know and are able to do so they become more effective—is a field manager's most important skill!

Each new manager needs to quickly, effectively, and permanently improve his/her teaching ability to get to the sixth level of conscious competent mentor.

Webster's dictionary describes mentor as a "wise advisor, a trusted teacher, or coach." Once a manager consciously learns and becomes a competent trainer of others, he or she must never slip into the unconscious mentor mode as shown in Figure 6–7; that is, teaching becomes rote and automatic: the results are sadly lacking.

SETTING SALES TRAINING PRIORITIES

In *The Sales Manager as a Trainer,* Rodger Davenport advises field sales managers to do the things with the highest payout. Teach must-know and need-to-know skills and knowledge first and you'll rarely get around to the nice-to-know. He advises:

"Train the successful salesperson . . . keep in mind that perhaps even those who do not necessarily need certain training in order to do an adequate or improved job can benefit greatly from training in certain areas, such as new products or polishing sales skills. This need is particularly true with the top 15 to 20 percent of your sales force—the people that you don't get around to working with very often because they tend to handle their own problems. When a new product comes out, these people study it themselves and go out and sell it. Or when

FIGURE 6–8

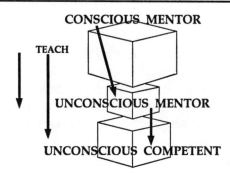

CONSCIOUS MENTOR

TEACH

UNCONSCIOUS MENTOR

UNCONSCIOUS COMPETENT

a new program is adopted, they get the basic information they need and then move on it on their own."

Davenport also points out that in not scheduling "work-withs" with these top producers, we rob them of two things: (1) higher motivation and success, and (2) the recognition they deserve. Every salesperson, regardless of level of expertise, can benefit from training; and these people especially can help train others.

Your leadership role as head of the district's sales force can be multiplied by training all, and encouraging each salesperson to share ideas and knowledge with others in the district. As shown in Figure 6–8, you must hone your own ability to teach—and teach others how to instruct. One major reason for doing this is that the instructor usually learns the most. Another reason is that the best transfer of knowledge takes place between the person most familiar with the job and the novice, that is, experienced reps training inexperienced reps.

HOW TO INSTRUCT

The one, surefire method of instruction is a simple, four-step operation for helping a person to learn a task.

Step One: *Prepare* the worker. Influence the attitude of the learner by preparing for the demonstration: explain the task and its importance, find out what the learner already knows. Inject knowledge by showing the finished product, stressing why it needs to be done correctly, and positioning the learner to see the demonstration just as the doer sees it. Get the learner to want to learn!

Step Two: *Present* **the material.** Move out in the knowledge dimension (and further build attitudes) by presenting the material, demonstrating it clearly, completely, and patiently. Tell, show, and illustrate one important step at a time, stressing each key point. A key point should be a reason why something is being done. Question understanding. Let the learner watch; test for understanding.

Step Three: *Try out* **performance.** Move up the skill dimension by having the trainee perform the operation while you coach, compliment, correct, and encourage. Your feedback and positive reinforcement keeps the trainee going; saying "OK" . . . , "good," . . . "that's right" lets them know they're on the right track. Have the trainee explain each key point to you as he or she does the job again. This feedback is essential so that you know the salesperson has absorbed what you have been teaching.

Step Four: *Follow through.* Extend the skill dimension (and subsequently the attitude) by showing you have confidence in their performance. As soon as you are sure the salesperson is doing the task right, leave him or her to practice: "OK, Mary, suppose you take this next call alone." After showing the learner how to get assistance, decrease supervision to normal amounts. Continue to check back with your sales staff and encourage questions.

This is the four-step method of training. Any job, no matter how complicated, can be broken down into simple tasks, or segments of the job. Each segment can be taught quickly by following these steps. When working with a new salesperson in making joint calls, you can have the sales rep concentrate on part of the call. Perform team selling, which allows you to demonstrate a particular step of the call or a technique you want to encourage the rep to use. In the car after the call, have the rep practice on you. Then have the rep perform that segment on all future calls. Have the rep practice more difficult parts of the job on each subsequent call. Oversimplified, the steps for training might be listed as follows:

1. Tell the rep what it is you are going to teach.
2. Demonstrate the skill to the rep.
3. Have the rep perform the skill.
4. Follow up.

How to Prepare to Train

1. Have a time table:
   Determine how much skill you expect him or her to have, and by when.
2. Break down the job:
   List important steps.
   Pick out the key points.
3. Have everything ready:
   Equipment, materials, and supplies.
4. Have the workplace properly arranged:
   Demonstrate how the salesperson will be expected to keep the workplace.

The Job Breakdown—Key to Effective Learning

A basic tool of instruction (discovered in industrial training more than fifty years ago) helps a manager organize instruction. It is called a job breakdown and has two essential elements: *steps* and *key points*. A step is a logical segment of operations to advance the performance of the work (the sequence in which work must be done); key points are those few critical points that, if overlooked, can make or break the performance of the job—the special skills or reasons why a step should be done in a certain way. The form shown in Figure 6–9, helps both instructor and student to readily grasp the operation being taught. List the steps of doing the task in the left column and match key points on the right.

Try completing Figure 6–9 for the closing of a sale on your number one product. For any task that you have had difficulty teaching in the past, just prepare a Job Breakdown for it. I guarantee your training effectiveness will double!

FIGURE 6–9
Closing the Sale on Your #1 Product: "_____"

Main Steps:	Key Points:
1.	•
2.	•
3.	•

WHEN DO YOU ACCOMPLISH FIELD SALES TRAINING?

Field sales training can and does take place any time, any place. You are doing sales training all the time. Every time you check over a salesperson's report, mark it up and return it; send a note; leave a message; talk to him or her on the phone; make a joint sales call; make a statement; answer a question; give the person something to read; demonstrate; take action with the person; criticize; compliment; check their work; talk with their customers or conduct a meeting—you are giving training. Sales training is continuous. Because it can do so much to affect current and future performance, you need to seize the opportunity wherever and whenever it presents itself.

WHERE FIELD SALES TRAINING CAN BE DONE

The Sales Rep's Car

The sales representative spends a good portion of his or her lifetime in an auto—from 14 to 30 percent of the working day, according to surveys of sales rep workshop participants. This time can be used effectively for training:

1. *Coach while you're a passenger in the sales representative's car.* It is usually most productive to accompany the sales representative in his/her car. This gives ample opportunity for discussion—to

make points, ask questions, check understanding, and listen! It also gives you a reading on how the sales rep organizes for selling. When setting up your training itinerary, arrange to meet the sales rep in the rep's territory early in the morning. Teach good work habits by example—go to the rep; don't ask the rep to go out of his/ her planned route to pick you up. (What you *do* thunders so loudly he/she cannot hear a word you say!) Get agreement before each call on what your respective roles will be during the call. Between calls, discussion (most likely to help the learning) can be stimulated by questions like: "Why do you suppose the customer . . .?" "How do you plan to . . .?" "What is the advantage of . . .?"

2. *Practice through role play.* While traveling between calls, have the sales representative practice giving sales presentations to you. You can do much to help the person improve selling skills by playing the role of the customer. Try to act as a real customer might: Offer objections, then critique and coach.

3. *Curbside critique.* One of the most effective ways to make a true learning experience out of your joint calls with your sales representatives is to conduct a thorough critique of each call. Through research of the appropriateness of positive reinforcement and negative correction of a salesperson, Robert Benford found:

a. Positive reinforcement spoken by the manager on a joint call immediately after the sales representative performs what the manager perceives as good has strong positive influence greatly enhancing the probability of the rep's repeating the same action in subsequent sales calls.

b. Corrective action spoken by the manager immediately after the sales representative does something bad or fails to do something good (in the manager's opinion), is usually perceived by the rep as negative criticism of a mistake and has little or no effect on future use by the sales representative of the manager's advice, but;

c. That same corrective action noted ("Let's see on our next call if we can learn from what just happened") and witheld until just prior to the next sales call, spoken by the manager as a suggestion: "Remember when we lost the sale? This time suppose you . . .", greatly enhances implementation and the continued use of the suggested (corrective) action.

That's an important lesson for a manager! It points out how everyone wants desperately to be right and the manager who helps his or her people to be right, also wins!

4. *Cassette player/recorder.* A small audiocassette tape recorder can be a useful training/supervision device used in the auto by the manager or by the trainee while traveling between calls. For purposes of training it can be used to play sample presentations, give information, play training tapes, record and play back practice sales presentations, and rehearse answers to tough objections some customers might offer. For purposes of supervision it can provide recorded instructions, and can serve the manager as a reminder and trip reporter. You should keep a separate cassette on each sales rep and, at the conclusion of a work-with, dictate a verbal report of the day's results, the areas worked on, additional training needs uncovered, what the rep has agreed to do, and how you plan to follow up. Then before your next session with that sales rep, replay your verbal report. It will refresh your memory concerning needed areas of improvement.

5. *Visual aids and reminders.* Think of the salesperson's car as a training/communication station. Print up training aids and reminders in a form specifically designed to fit over the auto's window visor or for attachment to a clipboard. A printed "pocket card" and pocket calendar are effective devices for subtle extension of sales training. Special equipment may offer you additional opportunities to help sales representatives learn while parked in their cars or on sales calls: lap-top computers, car phones, voice mail, portable video players.

The Customer's Place of Business

No place offers more opportunity for learning by the sales rep than right where the action is: the customer's place of business. But because of the need to get sales and not upset the client relationship of your customer, you must plan the joint customer call carefully. You can't just interrupt an important sales presentation to a big prospect with "excuse us while I train!"

Consider waiting time—how can you utilize it to train your sales rep? All those minutes in the customer's waiting room can be invested in meaningful training discussion rather than casually thumbing through old magazines.

Or consider the customer's plant—what can you point out to the trainee, from walking about the customer's place of business, that would teach something of value about the business or customer's needs? Most facilities reveal merchandising/service opportunities. You can teach alertness to customer needs on the job far better than you can in the classroom.

Your Company's Branch or Regional Office

Some field sales training might be done in the local branch office, depending on facilities, availability, and convenience to the trainee's territory. The advantages of this are:

1. No rental charge.
2. The trainee sees the "big picture" of what goes on behind the sales.
3. There is input from others (other managers, secretaries, order processors).
4. Convenience of supplies, samples, and sales tools.

You are fortunate if you have a room at the branch office suitable for group meetings or one-on-one training sessions. Coordinate your training to these facilities.

Plan with care. Many branch offices are not good places for effective sales training. There may be interference with sales administration or interruptions (phones, visitors, and mail). Another consideration is that of impressions. First impressions on new trainees can be lasting: therefore, unless the salesperson's primary objective is processing paperwork rather than selling, it is better to start the new person out with you in the field selling!

The Company's Centralized Training Facility

Fortunate, indeed, is the field sales manager who is located close to, and can use, the company's centralized training center. Most centers are designed to supplement the basic sales training done in the field by the field sales manager. Therefore, training center courses concentrate on training the field sales manager in how to train, and in professionalizing the selling skills of sales representatives (already productive) who have four months or even years of experience. Take full advantage of all the professional sales training help your company offers and make the sales/training department your partner.

Use prepared sales training materials and programs when they are available, and ask for help with material you need in the field.

A Hotel or Motel Room

The quiet and comfort of a hotel or motel room makes it a good place for discussion and study. During nonselling periods of the day, you might use the hotel/motel room for training work. But plan for it. Decide what can best be taught here, whether it is preparation for sales presentations, paperwork, company policies, or practice of office presentations. Consider what you need: A card table? Extra chairs? Order them ahead of time.

Sales training is the sales manager's job. To do it, the manager must coordinate the training with all the appropriate resources and facilities. Start today to improve your sales team's learning. Identify each sales rep's level of competency and gaps in attitudes, skills, and knowledge. Break down the job into tasks to be learned. Use the four steps of good instruction to narrow those gaps.

CHECKLIST

_____ Train each of your sales representatives right the first time.
_____ Devote enough quality on-the-job days with your people to satisfy your manager.
_____ Have a very good idea of each sales representative's strengths and gaps in necessary attitudes, skills, and knowledge?
_____ Instructing a person in how to perform their job: take them through preparation, presentation, application and then follow up.
_____ Improve your training competency.

REFERENCE

1. Much of the information regarding the Learning Cube first appeared in *The Learning Cube* by Ray Higgins, © 1982 by Armour-Dial, Inc., and is reprinted with permission.

Chapter Seven

How to Coach Effectively: Deliberately Assist to Improve

The Manager's Workshop on "Getting Work Done through People" was in its second day when I pulled up a chair for the consultant at the table dealing with Davidson's problem. "I'm in a fix!" said the young man, about to be transferred to field sales manager. "I'm being sent into the Jacksonville District to take over from former District Manager Yancy Smith. He's been demoted but is staying on as a sales representative." I could see concern written all over the brow of Dorman Davidson, the young manager. Davidson had been a manager only six months and had impressed management with his first district's results . . . so much so that they gave him the toughest supervisory problem in the company.

My heart did a quick flip-flop. Only a month earlier I had worked two days with Smith. He was covering both of the district's retail territories as well as the district's major key account (Smith's young rep had quit the same week that Smith released his non-producing old-timer). Though Smith was in his mid-50s, he had run my legs off for two days and sold more at both store and head-quarter's level than I ever dreamed possible. I had honestly reported back to management my impression of Smith as "the best salesperson I'd witnessed in the company; gave a most professional presentation to his key account"; but "is definitely a 'doer' and critical of other sales reps."

I'll never forget the next 30 minutes of discussion in that small group, as they wrestled with Dorman Davidson's problem of how to prevent Smith's resentment and build a successful sales team in his new district. We discovered this was Yancy Smith's second successive demotion—his former district had been divided into three districts, renamed Atlanta Zone, and a new zone manager was brought in. Everyone in the company knew Yancy from the president on down. He was a fiercely proud, energetic, and outspoken person. We disected and analyzed what we knew of the problem, zeroing in on how Yancy Smith must feel about any new (and especially a young) district manager taking over his former job. Davidson's problem got the full treatment of the scientific thought method and he and others in his group role-played how to do the initial face-to-face sit-down with Smith.

"Sing him about 40 verses of *'Oh, How I Need You!'*," the consultant said as he and I got up from the table.

The young manager did just that. Later, he told me of his first and subsequent coaching contacts with Smith: "The first thing I said to him was that I hadn't asked for the move; that I needed him a hundred times more than he needed me; and that all I asked was for him to give me a chance. I discovered that he had been passed over three times on deserved salary adjustments and so I went to bat for him and got him an immediate increase. Then I asked for his help in training a young, new sales rep—stressed how much the young man could learn from Yancy's experience— and he did an excellent job of training. In the first year, we busted all our sales budgets and earned maximum incentive."

The young sales manager gave as much attention to his senior sales rep as he did to his "rookie," regularly scheduling work with days with each for what he called mutual learning. From this district (that stretched from the city of Jacksonville through northern Florida and south Georgia), the three person sales team produced sales that amazed everyone. As business grew, another salesperson was employed, with senior rep Smith aiding the initial training. For the next 10 years the Jacksonville District far exceeded budgets, earned full incentives, and won most of the company's sales contests. I saw and heard much from Davidson and Smith for years. Funny thing was: Davidson always gave the credit for success to his ace, senior sales representative Yancy Smith, and to the other salespersons added to the district as it grew. Smith continued as top producing sales representative for another decade before retiring at age 70 (long after Davidson was promoted out of the district).

This manager used coaching to get results through people, while avoiding mistakes and making his sales budgets.

WHAT IS COACHING?

Coaching is any process by which a manager *deliberately* assists a subordinate to improve. That covers a lot. It includes all your deliberate assistance in contacts with your sales representatives, be it a telephone conversation, a message left in voice-mail, or in a note or marked-up piece of paper returned to the original sender; a face-to-face discussion, work with, a meeting with a group of your sales reps, or a formal sitdown with a rep to review annual performance.

The good coach gets out in the field. Coaching is a managerial skill that consists of the separate, but highly related performance of observation, analysis, demonstration, and feed-back of your observations to the salesperson. It requires getting out into the salesperson's territory to observe the salesperson in action. It is nearly impossible to analyze performance deficiencies accurately from call cards, trip reports, computer printouts, and other factual data alone.

It is commonly accepted that coaching is one of the most, if not *the* most, important ways by which a field manager stimulates the development of his or her sales representatives.

Definitions of Coaching

Many forms of coaching are necessary, so let's define them. Some will be dealt with in this chapter, others in subsequent chapters.

Informal coaching—sometimes called day-to-day coaching—where the manager observes a sales rep performing job responsibilities or skills in a particular manner and indicates his or her approval or disapproval. Includes setting an example (by the manager). It is here, in day-to-day operations on the job, that most development takes place!

Formal coaching—sometimes called annual coaching—a scheduled appraisal or coaching interview usually conducted following a review of current performance. This periodic Preventive Maintenance Check-up of over-all performance aids realism in understanding between manager and sales rep if it answers: "What results did we get," "Why we got those results," "What can we learn from it to help in the period ahead," and "What will we do?"

Both formal and informal coaching are necessary for success! The real purpose of scheduled or formal coaching is to supplement the coaching that goes on day-to-day.

Group coaching—a form of informal coaching such as a district meeting to deal with operating problems or to conduct group training—affecting the attitudes, skills, and knowledge of several sales reps in a group setting. Properly planned and executed, meetings save time by efficient sharing and training of many reps at one time.

Tactical coaching—a positive response to an improvement opportunity that is presently occurring. (Usually short range, seizing an improvement for getting today's business.)

Strategic coaching—planning your coaching activities in advance of a visit with a sales rep. (Usually aimed at longer term development of the rep's attitude, skill, and knowledge. Might include planning a sequence of developmental experiences.)

WHY COACH?

Effective coaching is a "must" if the corporation is to get better business results year after year. Your district is expected to turn in improved productivity, often times without the benefit of additional resources, that is, people. Thus, you've got to improve the team's productivity through coaching the team members to become even better than they were before.

Coaching is one of the most effective tools a manager has to make a difference in the performance of his or her district. It is your job. Your company expects you to coach. Your people expect to be coached. Yet, many managers resist coaching—especially coaching with greater frequency or with greater effectiveness. *Why do managers resist coaching?* Because of:

1. Work pressure.
2. Reluctance to criticize an experienced rep.
3. Lack of useful tools and techniques.

4. "Sink or swim" philosophy.
5. Lack of confidence in handling "delicate" discussions.
6. "Me versus you" attitude.

Improving coaching practices requires busy managers to change; it requires doing both formal and informal coaching and being proactive in your coaching!

But just look at what that can do for you. I had a group of 24 district managers in the food industry survey 79 of their subordinates on 15 questions like "How well do you know what is expected of you in your job?", "How satisfied are you with your supervision?". Fifty-eight of the 79 subordinates reported their district managers conducted "regular systematic interviews" on performance and 21 of the 79 subordinates reported they "never had a formal interview" (27 percent). The results were:

- 84 percent of those with interviews said, "My supervisor motivates me to do my best job in appropriate or very appropriate ways," and only 43 percent of those not interviewed gave these positive answers.
- 72 percent of those interviewed said, "I always or usually get the recognition and encouragement I deserve," and only 43 percent of those not interviewed gave these answers.
- 64 percent of those interviewed said, "My supervisor gives me considerable assistance or goes out of his way to help me do a better job," and only 38 percent of those not interviewed gave this answer.
- 88 percent of those interviewed said, "I have a very good idea or know exactly what is expected of me," and only 62 percent of those not interviewed gave this answer.
- 88 percent of those interviewed said, "My supervisor supervises me about right; he directs my activities but still gives me enough leeway," and only 57 percent of those not interviewed answered in this way, while 38 percent complained of being supervised "too loosely" or "far too loosely."

The supervisor who sees value in providing regular interviews is seen by his or her subordinates as an individual who is likely to:

- Let him/her know what is expected.
- Let him/her know how they stand.

- Supervise him/her about right.
- Provide frank statements about his or her performance.
- Provide suggestions and assistance when needed.
- Utilize appropriate motivational methods.

HOW TO COACH

Coach on the basis of results. Stress results, not personal traits. Start with the positives (strengths). Make criticism job centered, that is, use correction as clearly a learning experience, emphasizing the "Let's learn from that so that the next time we encounter that, try to . . ."

The field sales manager described at the beginning of this chapter had been told (in vivid terms) by previous supervisors of senior rep Smith about Yancy's "cantankerous personality." But the manager chose to ignore that and build on strengths. He set frequent short-range challenges and the long-range goal of "best district in the nation and best individual production record in the company for Smith"; and constantly kept all his reps posted on their progress.

Compare these two statements from inside the shoes of the sales rep:

1. "Let's figure out a way to plan our next call. The planning of that last sales call could have been better in which two areas?"
2. "You are a poor planner; you've just got to become a better planner!"

The second statement personalizes the problem and produces defensiveness and frustration. Better to state the problem in operational terms—in terms of results.

Remember what it's like to be on the receiving end. When you were a sales rep, wouldn't you have worked to improve the planning of your calls—but fought or resented being reformed?

Get down to cases. Give timely assistance by reviewing plans and sales strategies by the rep before going into an account.

When you spot an opportunity for the rep to improve, don't be general, vague, or hint around about a problem. Get down to cases. Be specific. Ask the rep if he/she sees a better way. Use incidents as they occur to get a point across. Give reasons for your opinions. Be frank, but open. Good managers use these five "F"s: Friendly, Frank, Factual, Fair, and Firm.

Determine causes. Avoid the reaction: "Something is wrong; what are you going to do about it?" Ask *why* are these results not satisfactory? . . . what's causing this? *All Behavior is Caused*—explore reasons behind poor results (that's the "A-B-Cs" of managing people). Then, give 'em *help,* not hell!

Here are three reasons why your correction of a salesperson may fail to get results:

1. The sales rep *doesn't know* (understand) what's expected.
2. The sales rep knows what's expected but *doesn't know how* to correct the shortcoming.
3. The sales rep *doesn't want to* follow through.

Discuss it in a two-way process. Use a joint problem-solving process. Real development is stimulated when you both try to realistically discuss the results which have or have not been achieved. Have a give-and-take discussion. Be sure not to dominate.

Use questions effectively. Constructive questions are your most powerful tool to cause acceptance. Questions that make the sales rep analyze "results" produce more change than admonitions, platitudes, and edicts. Ask for the sales rep's perception. This helps you see where the rep is coming from and helps diagnose if the problem is a skill or attitude issue.

Provide for self-correction. Pin down precise goals that the rep will fight to meet and by which he/she will be able to gauge progress. The important thing is to help the sales representative to better performance. Motivate by jointly developing targets. Do not impose them. Challenge. Get him or her to change harmful habits and improve by self-direction.

An example of how powerful precise goals can be in providing self-direction came out in a recent managers' workshop: I had relented and allowed one company to include (as a participant) a high potential salesperson with the other eighteen managers. While discussing manager's techniques for motivating the reps to follow through, one manager said, "I'd like to ask the sales rep present what he responds to."

The rep turned in his chair, smiled, and answered: "You know, in my company my district manager sends out a weekly posting of where we stand on each of the common sales goals. On that one sheet of paper are rankings for all ten of us on each category of achievement. It is *so* embarrassing to be last. I—and every rep in the district—try my darndest to avoid being on the bottom on any item so I sell like hell! All these other ideas about coaching don't have near the impact of peer pressure!"

Set up a developmental sequence. The major reason a sales rep plateaus in performance is from lack of newness in the job. As the rep's manager, you can aid his or her growth by planning the rep's sequence of exposure to new skills, new knowledge, and different opinions. Plan so each is exposed to progressively more responsible work through special assignments, work withs, reading, added responsibilities, and training.

To implement these how-to's of coaching, you will need to get out into each rep's territory and work with the individual.

Figure 7–1 shows a visual pattern of a manager's work with.

THE COACHING MODEL

When you see a reason to offer coaching, do it in a timely manner—discuss it as close to the incident as practical, while details are still fresh before the impact of feedback dies. With positive reinforcement, do it immediately; with negative (correction), do it in private and call attention to the action as an opportunity for future improvement: "Sally, I want you to remember the way you tried to close because I think I can help you try it differently on our next call." Then deal with it as close to try-out time as you can. But don't nit-pick. Consider the overall perfor-

FIGURE 7–1
The 'Work With' Coaching Cycle

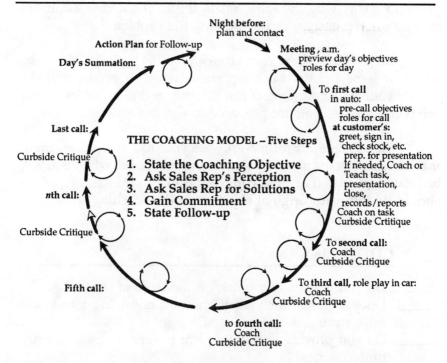

mance, not extremes. Focus on important aspects of the job. And deal only constructively with observable behavior that impacts job performance. Here is an effective way to do it.

Step One: *State the coaching objectives.* When you have a reason to offer coaching (you see poor call planning, low closing ratio, insufficient number of sales calls, or difficulty handling objections), explain the specific objectives for the coaching session.

Step Two: *Ask for the salesperson's perception.* Ask "How do you see it?"

Probe to see where the sales rep is coming from, if he/she recognizes the problem and its seriousness. This helps you to diagnose skill, knowledge, or attitude. If no recognition of the need to change is shown, tell what bothers you and why it is important to you. Probe for why it exists. Listen actively.

Step Three: *Get the salesperson to come up with solutions.* If acceptable, go on to getting commitment. If not acceptable, probe to clarify why the salesperson thinks it could work. If appropriate, offer assistance in resolving the problem.

Step Four: *Gain commitment.* What will be done by when. It is best if the sales rep states what he or she will do. Clarify your understanding of the solution and gain commitment. Tell consequences you are prepared to use if not done.

Step Five: *State follow-up.* Set your follow-up date. Summarize what is to be done, by whom and when. Tell when you will be following up and express your confidence in the sales rep. This should tie into your original objective of the coaching session.

CHECKLIST

_____ Do you deliberately coach on the basis of results?

_____ Do you give timely assistance by reviewing plans and sales strategies by your reps?

_____ Do you provide encouragement to reps on their difficult undertakings?

_____ Do you use questions to bring out, identify, and build understanding of underlying causes before asking the rep for his or her solutions?

_____ Have you provided suggestions and other assistance when needed by your sales representatives?

Chapter Eight

How to Reinforce Performance

One problem faces every sales manager: getting people to do what you want them to do, that is, do the right things and do them the right way. You may have trained your sales representatives as well as you know how; followed the guidelines of the previous chapter in your coaching contacts; exhorted them with all the reasons why; and still they are not doing what you want them to do. Why won't they?

Perhaps there are several reasons. Human nature demands that we be drawn to good and avoid that which we interpret as bad. That leads to a basic principle of performance: *The things that get done are the things that get rewarded.*

OFFERING REWARDS

A corollary: If you aren't getting the things you want, find out what is being rewarded. Or, better still, find out how your sales reps perceive those "rewards" they receive. Here are a few simple examples:

Your sales rep sells more and is given a bigger budget.

The rep who sells the most is given the toughest accounts.

The fast worker's reward may be that he or she is given more work to do! You know what they say: "If you want a job done, find a busy person and give them the job."

To some, this is an appropriate reward. They relish the challenge. To others this is not a reward but a punishment! They find if they work slower, they are rewarded with less work. Thus, if the reward isn't worth the effort, it becomes more rewarding to either not do it or do it in a perfunctory way.

A basic saying of supervision is: Subordinates do what their managers inspect (with consequences applied), not (necessarily) what they expect! Which beings us back to the premise that the things that get done are the things that get rewarded.

Is there a solution? Yes, but it is easier said than done. A manager is supposed to balance the consequences which means increased reward for good performance and/or decreased reward for bad performance.

The trick is how to do this. The tangible rewards you can offer are:

- Salary increases.
- Promotion.
- Prizes.
- Bonuses.

Your tangible reward options are very limited.

Suppose you have six sales reps. As the district manager, you can't offer the lure of promotion to all six. It's great to have a couple of truly promotable management candidates. It's a cruel hoax to offer potential promotion as a reward falsely. This is a real and ongoing dilemma in field sales.

Sales managers grope for appropriate rewards to balance the consequences and create an environment where motivated people can flourish. Many years ago in our first new managers' training class I was asked "How can I motivate my salespeople?" I don't know how you might answer that question, but, somewhat at a loss, I answered, "You don't motivate people; motivation is an inner drive. You hire motivated people and then, don't do anything to *de*motivate them." Now, years later, when this subject comes up, I give the same answer. What we address in "Motivational Training" is how to keep winners motivated to go on winning.

Intangible Rewards

Tangible rewards are limited but, there are *intangible* rewards which management can offer to people to enable them to draw satisfaction from work well done. These rewards include recognition, praise, and approval. We all work so much better when we get real satisfaction from the work.

However, our work may be somewhat less than excellent when we see it as drudgery, something we have to do just to get through the day. Think of all the stereotypes of the '9-to-5' syndrome, the "rat race." How much excellence can we expect when people feel that way about work? When we are doing what we like we don't really want to stop. When work is drudgery, time is a plague.

USING POSITIVE REINFORCEMENT AS A MOTIVATIONAL TOOL

Well, what can you, as manager, do about this? None of us is naive enough to think there is a magic key we can turn to achieve excellence and productivity. How can you restore some balance to the consequences of your sales representatives' work, and increase the intangible rewards by at least a little?

We suggest that if you improve your use of positive reinforcement to stimulate latent motivation you can restore some balance to the consequences of work performance. Positive reinforcement is not very new but like the weather, we all talk about it while little is done about it.

Many managers, having learned a little about positive reinforcement, will say to their subordinate: "Nice call, good presentation, keep up the good work."

In performance appraisals we have all been taught to talk about the good things first and then, point out the bad things.

Still, a simple pat on the back is not precisely what is meant by positive reinforcement. It is much more and demands good listening skills and productive engagement of an intellect. You have to observe what has taken place and think about it if you are to positively reinforce good performance and set the stage for correcting performance discrepancies.

Let's dig a little into the listening part. Why must you listen? To give praise—or reinforcement—you must understand precisely *why* the performance is good and play this back to the person. For example, you might say:

John, I was impressed with the way you conducted that sales call, you opened with a question to make sure you were focusing on the customer's real need and then, selected features and benefits which underscored the need the buyer considered important.

The point is you have to tell why it was well done to project sincerity and to let them know you really are paying attention. I can almost guarantee that if you habitually reinforce good performance, in this way, it will be repeated.

Skip the "You're doing great, keep up the good work" pat-on-the-back. After a short time that will not sound sincere. To make it stick you have to tell them why you found the performance well done.

There is an interesting and valuable book by Mager and Pipe called *Analyzing Performance Problems* (Lear-Siegler). It talks about "performance discrepancies" and asks the question "Is it a training problem?" . . . Is the missing performance due to a lack of skill? A lack of knowledge? Maybe both? If you find this out by asking yourself "If this person's life depended on it, could he or she do it?" and if the answer is "No," then indeed it *is* a training problem.

For example—Harvard Graphics on the computer; why can't I do it? Because I lack knowledge and skill, therefore, it's a training problem. If my life depended on it I couldn't *do* it. I would need training.

Let's say, however, that I had been trained and I used to do a fair job of producing work on Harvard Graphics. *But,* now I'm late, sloppy, and don't seem very enthusiastic. *Not* a training problem; it's motivation and this brings us face-to-face with perceived rewards, or, right back to balancing the consequences. You can threaten me with loss of my job and I will do just enough to get by, but I won't be as good as I can be. Lousy for me and for my employer.

Another helpful book is *The One Minute Manager* by Blanchard and Johnson (Morrow Co.). This book is the best thing I know of to help you learn *How To*—how to use positive reinforcement to help people draw satisfaction from the work itself and thus do superior work for their companies, large or small.

The lesson of *The One Minute Manager* is that, as a manager, you have to create an environment which helps individual motivation flourish. The following quote from the book offers a good summary of these points.

"The One Minute Praising works well when you:

1. Tell people up front that you are going to let them know how they are doing.
2. Praise people immediately.
3. Tell people what they did right—be specific.
4. Tell people how good you feel about what they did right, and how it helps the organization and other people who work here.
5. Stop for a moment of silence to let them "feel" how good you feel.
6. Encourage them to do more of the same.
7. Shake hands or touch people in a way that makes it clear that you support their success in the organization."

This book became famous for the phrase you may still hear, "Catch people doing something right" (as opposed to catching them doing something wrong) and instructs us to reward them on the spot—an obvious truth but so often overlooked in our hectic lives.

Field sales managers must get out into his or her sales reps' territories to observe *what's right* and *what's not* and apply appropriate positive reinforcement. Positive reinforcements, from simplest to more severe, include: Show expressions of pleasure, a smile, nodding of the head, handshake, touch on the shoulder, high-fives; Praise, spoken thanks and words of encouragement; Ask them to serve as a model to others, to teach their techniques to others, and help build our winning team; Relate their action to forthcoming appraisal; Written commendation, note of thanks, posting or publication of accomplishment; Buy them coffee, take them to lunch; Commendation before peers, letter of thanks from your boss or top brass, recognition award; Prize, bonus, title, promotion, pay—these are but a few of the positive reinforcements available. There are opposites for most of them; negative consequences that you can apply, from subtle to more severe: a frown; showing an expression of displeasure, pointing out the effect on his/her reputation—"This is not the quality sales job you are capable of, Mary"; "I'm disappointed, John, you are a much better sales rep than that"—to a chewing out in private, written warning, or other disciplinary action. These negative reinforcements may be used *constructively* when appropriate. They are not nearly as effective as positives.

So, positive reinforcement is the key both to training and to motivation. Little rewards, or, reinforcements, help us to learn initially and then to develop experience in a skill or families of skills. I've heard these referred to as *skill clusters*. This is how people learn and develop increasing levels of competence.

I urge you to work at your positive reinforcement, look for sales reps doing something right, improve the rewards system by giving specific praise. A little improvement pays off with big results.

I am told that the best you can hope for when you write—or talk to a group—is that they might remember three things you said. Let me suggest these three as worth your effort:

1. The things that get done are the things that get rewarded.
2. When you reward someone with praise, be specific and tell them *why* the performance was well done.
3. People learn and will be motivated to keep learning if they are frequently rewarded with *positive reinforcement*.

People's behavior will gradually change one step at a time in the direction of the reward.

CHECKLIST

_____ Have you provided your reps with timely praise and recognition in very specific terms for jobs well done?

_____ Are your sales reps assured of receiving timely and appropriate discipline when it is deserved?

_____ Are your discussions of performance with each rep matter-of-fact and businesslike? Are you specific in expressing your opinions?

Chapter Nine

How to Question and Listen

Efforts to improve your skills of questioning and listening will aid you in performing your three main roles as field manager. These basic roles, *problem solving, communicating,* and *follow through* are obvious from our studies of thousands of field managers.

Does your job consist of identifying, analyzing, and solving problems? Communicating with your sales force (down, up, sideways, and diagonally through your organization)? Seeing to it that the sales job is performed? If so, mastering the questioning and listening tools shown in this chapter will help.

In Chapter 2 we quoted from *Help me, Don't tell me! A Guidebook To Motivating Sales Performance.* In the booklet's Introduction, Don Waite, president of Sales Staff Surveys, Inc. says:

"Our company, Sales Staff Surveys, Inc., was created to help management listen to their sales staff's opinions on how to improve selling effectiveness. In doing so, we accumulated a massive amount of qualitative and quantitative data from over 25,000 sales representatives who responded to their companies' opinion surveys. Regardless of industry, they tell us a consistent story of what not only motivates performance but also what demotivates performance."

On two-way communication, CEO Waite reports:

"Our research has confirmed that motivation increases when reps know what is expected, feel their ideas and opinions are respected, and receive feedback on performance. Thus *communication becomes the catalyst which brings the manager and rep together* [italics mine]. The resulting teamwork can then achieve mutually set goals."

This is good advice. Yes, communication is the glue, the binder that holds your district together. Your staff members are probably much like the 25,000 sales representatives who responded to his clients' opinion surveys. Therefore, we will structure this chapter around sales reps' responses that fall under the following four headings:

1. Where Communication Breaks Down.
2. Ways You Can Improve.
3. Listening Is Your First Step.
4. Motivational Tips.

We will follow the reproduced quotes (permission of Sales Staff Surveys) of the sales representatives with *How-To's* from NSSTE sales management trainers. Here's how you can develop and improve your own skills of questioning and listening to motivate more effectively.

WHERE COMMUNICATION BREAKS DOWN

In listing concerns which affect their sales effectiveness and reasons for lack of job satisfaction, reps identify poor communication as a demotivator. Here are typical examples:

District manager is a poor listener so communication is difficult.

District manager seldom communicates new information.

If I want to know what's going on within the company, I have to contact other people in my district.

Communication to and from my district manager is at a minimum.

I get more information from reps in another district where the manager is more open and trusting.

I need to talk with my manager in detail about aspects of the job that could help me and help the company without fear of ridicule.

While most of us would not admit to frequently making mistakes in talking to people, we all do. I well remember having written a booklet on "Listening" (for managers) only to have my spouse of many years ask me: "How come *you* never read this?" Communication is one of the most talked about, yet least understood and practiced, skill *everyone needs*. No manager is so skilled in communicating with his or her people that conscious training and practice in interviewing wouldn't help improve.

Oftentimes, the harder one tries to persuade another, the more the other's resistance stiffens. Some managers make common mistakes in trying to "motivate" sales representatives only to *de*motivate them. This occurs when the sales rep comments and the manager reacts by:

Interrupting.
Not really listening.
Assuming he/she knows what the rep means.
Giving advice.
Passing judgment for or against the view expressed.
Belittling.
Threatening, whether implied or real.

Three Key Lessons from Communication Breakdowns

1. *To communicate, a manager must listen.* "Telling" is not communicating. What is important is not what you—the manager—tells, it is what the employee accepts! You have to really believe that the employee has it within him/herself, if helped to see the problem clearly, to find the satisfactory solution. This requires *active listening* on the manager's part.

2. *Both parties—manager and salesperson—are in the discussion to gain.* Win-win strategy is the only consistently successful way to persuade. Both you and the sales rep want to profit from the discussion. Recognize this and point out to the rep that you are there to help and that, in doing so, you help them help you and their district.

3. *Avoid threat.* Real or implied, threats and undue pressure cause the other person to react defensively; to prepare rebuttal and return the threat. This "threat-defense-threat mechanism" is a law of human nature. It was explained by communication guru Hayakawa many years ago, when he said: "Self-concept (way I see it) tends to rigidify under conditions of threat . . . when shouting starts, communication ends."

WAYS YOU CAN IMPROVE

The following examples are sales representatives' suggestions for improving communications (taken from Waite's surveys):

> Require management at all levels to listen to the problems of the territory sales rep.
>
> Improve field management's understanding of field needs by taking more time to listen.
>
> I need to know what we are trying to achieve and the strategy to get there.
>
> It is tough to communicate bad news without being punished.

If you carefully read the two preceding chapters, "Coaching" and "Positive Reinforcement," you realize that both are about gaining acceptance or, more specifically, "getting your salespeople to do what you want them to do." In every NSSTE sales managers' workshop the subject of motivation comes up. Usually, it is expressed along the lines of "How do I motivate them to do what I want done?"

What are a manager's best tools for motivating or persuading? How does one person persuade another? The answer is to use skills that build two-way confidence. To negotiate a win-win resolution. There is no one big thing you can do to "motivate" other human beings; but there are a whole lot of little things you will do skillfully if your attitude is right (toward helping your employees) and you practice—causing them to motivate themselves. After all, it is not what you tell your people that counts, it is what they accept. The decision to do what you want them to do must come from within each salesperson.

Use Leadership and Persuasion

General Dwight D. Eisenhower (when he was supreme commander of the Allied Forces in Europe) defined Leadership as: "the ability to get other people to do what you want done because They want to do it!" Thus, persuasion is at the core of leadership.

Skills that Build Two-way Confidence

You have already reviewed some of these necessary skills. Problem solving or "Decision Thinking" is one of three necessary sets of skills as discussed in Chapter 3. Questioning and Listening are the other two. (We partially covered the later two in the chapters on Coaching and Selection Skills, but not all the tools of questioning and listening.) Blend the three sets of skills together (Decision Thinking, Questioning, and Listening) and you will show the hallmarks of effective managers as persuaders.

KNOW YOUR TOOLS AND HOW TO USE THEM

A skilled master knows all the tools available in his/her profession and skillfully blends their use, picking the right tool to fit each step of the task. In communication, for example, telling is a tool. Like a hammer. But not too many cabinetmakers go to work with only a hammer. As revealed by what sales reps say about their managers (Sales Staff Surveys), *de*motivation results from being treated like nails ("hammered on" by the district manager)! Let's look at *all* the tools at your disposal. An inventory may reveal some in your toolbox that you've neglected too long.

Tools of Questioning and Listening

You've used many of them all through life. But, unlike professionally trained psychiatrists, psychologists, and counselors, many managers have never known each tool by name; understood its use; and had formal training and practice in the use of each tool. As a result, managers miss opportunities to make their contacts with their people most effective.

Let's briefly review problem solving to see how you might improve your questioning and listening skills to do effective *joint* problem solving. Why? Simply because you get the best results by guiding your sales reps to "discover" reasons for the thing you want done. Skilled questioning and listening can guide your sales representative through sound decision thinking to where the rep can make his/her own sound decision.

Problem Solving. Problem-solving skills (described in Chapter 4) provide a mental thought process through which you can apply your listening and questioning skills to lead the other party to 1) "Discover" the what, when, where, and who, 2) define the key question, and 3) work out the how and why (benefits) of doing what you want done. This track of thought flows:

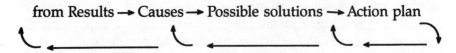

from Results → Causes → Possible solutions → Action plan

But remember it is a fluid process, with many cognitive eddies, that may require circling the problem several times before arriving at commitment to a suitable action plan. By keeping this thought structure in your mind, you can direct questioning that causes the discussion to move logically toward a mutually acceptable solution and plan.

Share problem discussion with individuals or groups of sales people. Skilled questioning and active listening works equally well in your one-on-one joint problem-solving interviews or in your group problem-solving meetings.

QUESTIONING

A question is the most powerful tool of teaching. The power of the question lies in the fact that *it compels an answer.* The questioning tools, used skillfully, help both the questioner and the questioned to think logically. Ask the right questions and you compel the right answers.

Let's discuss seven different types of questioning tools.

Constructive Questions

The first principle (or tool) in asking questions is that the question be used in a helpful manner and not to spy or degrade. Use constructive questions. Avoid questioning in a "third degree" or put-down manner. Always focus questions on the problem in a spirit of helpfulness. Avoid questions which imply criticism or threat—they only turn the power of the question against you, cause you to be confronted with a closed mind (opposition tends to close the mind), friction, and lack of cooperation.

Fact-Finding Questions

Ask lots of WHAT, WHY, WHEN, HOW, WHERE and WHO questions. They get you the facts and keep the employee's mind focused on the problem:

> What is the problem as you see it? Why is it a problem? When is it most prevelant? Why then? What would you say is the primary cause? What then is the real problem? What might we do about it? How else might it be done? Where? When? Whom might that affect? What would be the possible consequences?

"W" questions (even 'how' has a "w" in it) help the sales rep to see the whole problem. Ask the right questions and you can get the other party to come up with reasons for doing the thing you want done.

Justifying Questions

These questions get the other person to explain further. They are "go-deeper" questions. They ask for *reasons why, examples, evidence,* or *explanations:*

> "Could you give me an example of the close you used, Mary?"
>
> "Why do you suppose the buyer resisted?"
>
> "How was that?"
>
> "In what way, Tom?"
>
> "What is your basis for such a claim?"

Because this type of question could put the rep on the defensive, you should use it in a manner that is clearly helpful toward mutual understanding.

Return Questions

Get your people to answer their own questions. Of course it is so easy to give a quick answer—but usually much better to turn around the question: "What should I do, boss?" by responding:

"You're closer to this territory, Jay, what do you think you should do?"

"Well, what do you recommend?"

"It's your account, John, how might you resolve it?"

Putting the monkey on the sales rep's back by asking their recommended solutions helps get him/her to think logically and solve the rep's own problems. This helps you see where the rep is coming from so further questioning can lead the rep logically through the problem.

Hypothetical Questions

To introduce a new idea, bring up an overlooked point, give information, break a deadlock, or raise a possible course of action, use the "Suppose . . .; What?" or "Hypothetical" question. Like sending up a trial balloon, you state the possibility (as though you aren't certain of it) and ask the rep his/her opinion as to HOW it might work or WHAT we might learn from that information. You mention the possibility and ask for the salesperson's evaluation of the possibility:

"I'm wondering, just suppose you did . . .? How might you go about making that work?"

"What would be the advantages?"

Other examples could be:

"Over in Mary's territory, she handled it by doing . . . (such and such) "Any way you could adapt that here?" "How?"

"Suppose you told the buyer . . .? How might he react to that?"

The important thing is that you are not telling the rep how to do it, but rather raising a possibility for the rep to decide. You follow the new information or hypothetical case with HOW, WHAT,

WHY, WHEN, WHERE, or WHO (evaluative questions). By forcing the rep to evaluate the possibility, the rep's evaluation buys ownership for the idea. On the other hand, if you simply advise: "Why don't you . . .?"; the rep feels no ownership for the idea and follow through will be half-hearted and minimal. We are all loyal to those things we help to create or improve!

Alternative Questions

Your sales experience taught you this one a long time ago. You may have known it as the "Either/or" or "Alternative-choice" question. It is the technique of offering choices of "to-buy-or-to-buy". You ask the sales representative to choose between two or more possibilities, any of which you are willing to accept. Offer several solutions in the form of a question:

> Since I've got to have your numbers by four o'clock, which would be more convenient—for you to dig them out now while I wait, or call them to me about three this afternoon?

Summarizing Questions

Wrap up a discussion by a question or two on what's been accomplished through the conversation and what it is leading to. (Even if no agreement has been reached to this point in the discussion, agreeing on what you and the rep still disagree on is progress!) Examples:

> "Well, I'm glad we had this meeting, Jane. As a result, what is one thing you plan to do differently?"

> "Let's see if we understand this, number one; you will . . ., and two, I am going to help by . . . is that about it?"

Each of these questioning tools, Constructive, Fact-finding, Justifying, Return, Hypothetical, Alternative, and Summarizing encourages open-ended responses.

You should avoid questions that suggest a "yes" or "no" answer ("Closed" questions), except for confirmation. As you reviewed this inventory of questioning *tools*, which ones did you decide you need most to improve?

Your answers: Why selected?   How will you use it?

- _____   _____   _____
- _____   _____   _____

LISTENING IS YOUR FIRST STEP

A field manager's communication skills do motivate, as illustrated by reasons reps give for being "Very Satisfied" with their jobs:

New district manager is a motivator. Open communications with his employees.

Immediate manager listens and is making good attempts to respond to sales force's needs and problems.

I have a very good district manager; provides excellent support and has good listening skills, innovative suggestions. He delivers whatever he promises and will go to bat for me.

Excellent district manager . . . receive excellent feedback and training through her.

Listening should be an *active* process. Yet, many times we listen passively when a salesperson is talking. Perhaps it is because our minds are capable of processing thoughts at a much faster rate than most humans speak. So our minds fill-in with other thoughts. And the rest of our body gives us away. We glance at our watch, shift our feet, shuffle some paper, or fold our arms. And the sales rep notices. Apathy sets in.

How much better if we use the listening skills of managers cited above by their sales reps!

We all think we listen pretty well. We *don't*, most of the time. Have you noticed how much has been written about "listening" (from Ben Franklin right down to today's authors on persuasion, negotiation skills, and winning strategies)? Yet, time after time, we blow it.

More than one sales manager will read about the importance of listening to his or her reps, but, in the heat of supervision, the same manager will interrupt, dish out advice, and cut off discussion by the sales rep. That manager alone is unaware of the seething dissatisfaction or resignation that is building within the sales rep. I saw a high level manager kill all discussion in a session he (the manager) had titled "Operation Feedback." After asking the assembled troops for "an example of a unique way to approach a buyer," one brave sales rep told what the rep thought was pretty unique, only to be put down with:

Aw, that's not a new idea, we did that years ago in Philadelphia; I want to hear only *good* ideas!

That was the last rep to speak in "Operation Feedback." Try as he might, the manager could not coax another idea from his troops. (They sat quietly for 20 minutes until the manager dismissed the meeting early.)

What then, are specific Listening tools?

To your toolbox of the seven Questioning tools, you may want to add these seven Listening tools: Empathy; Neutrality; Proof of Listening; Clarifying; Restatement; Reflective; and Summarizing.

Empathy

Active, or real listening is shown more by your actions than any words you may use. An attitude of helpful listening displays empathy. Empathy is the ability to appreciate the other person's feelings—to share in another's emotions, thoughts, and feelings—without becoming so emotionally involved that your judgment is affected. It is akin to sympathy, but more like the listening-with-understanding of a strong friend that helps the person see his/her situation in perspective. This requires of the manager an ability to understand *why* the sales rep feels as she/he does, *how* she/he got that way and to *help* the rep see the problem in perspective to solve it.

Neutrality in Listening

The tool of neutrality defuses the "threat-defense-threat mechanism" and allows you to stay in control of the discussion. To use it, you reflect an attitude of complete neutrality, showing respect for the sales rep's point of view. Listen without moralizing; don't show shock, surprise, or opposition. Do not pass judgment on the "rightness" or "wrongness" of the reps view. In effect you tell the sales representative by your attitude: "It's all right to talk, I won't laugh at you." This helps the rep get the problem out, since you show an attitude of really wanting to hear and wanting to help.

By remaining neutral and checking your own tendency to jump in with advice, you force the rep to think. On the other hand, displaying a flat-footed judgment does much to wreck what could be constructive discussion. Here's why:

1. *You continue control* of the discussion and can focus it on analyzing the problem if you remain completely neutral and force the employee to continue talking.

2. *There is no control* of the discussion when you oppose, criticize, give advice, or pass moral judgment against the employee because the employee's mind will thoroughly close. On the defensive, the employee is likely not to hear a word you say!

3. *The employee may seize control* of the discussion when you state a moral judgment committing yourself to that person's position. This is especially dangerous when other people may be involved and before you have all facts and sides of the story.

You can do effective joint problem solving if you remain neutral. Don't take sides. Try to understand the sales rep. Try to find out how the rep feels. Keep the rep talking. Get all the facts you can. Display calmness. Focus the attention on the problem, not on personalities. Show your interest and desire to help—but no judgment please!

Proof of Listening

Show you want to hear, want to understand, want to help. Give complete attention with your eyes, facial expressions, body language, and occassional gutteral response. This tool is sometimes called the "Uh-huh Technique." You give proof that you are really listening by responses like: "Uh-huh . . . I see"; "Hmm"; "I understand"; "Uh-huh." A pause, and periods of silence are important tools of the interviewer. These pauses and audible expressions of interest, nodding of the head, and attention with the eyes keeps the sales rep talking and may dredge up important facts and feelings that might not otherwise be revealed.

Be patient. If the sales rep is troubled, he/she may go around in verbal circles. Deep feelings are hard to express even when one is not troubled. Be willing to tolerate some repetition or vagueness or periods of silence. Wait the rep out. You may find it appropriate at some point to ask, "How do you feel about talking with me?"

Clarifying

The "go deeper" tool of listening is used to try to get the sales rep to fully express him/herself. Part body language and part question, it probes for more information:

"Oh, how's that?" (puzzled expression).
"Err, can you give me a for-instance?"
"Such as . . .?"
"In what way is that a problem?"
"I don't understand . . . (pause) . . .?"
"Explain that."
"Are there any other things in addition to that?"
"Let me see if I understand you. You mean . . .?"

Use probing to get at causes or underlying problems. Try to clarify just what is the problem. The *clarifying* tool is aided by the use of *justifying* questions. This involves asking the sales rep about his/her statements.

Restatement

Restate the rep's words and *listen*. Repeating a phrase or a few key words spoken by your sales rep, and then waiting for an explanation is a helpful way to let the rep know you've been listening and want to know more. This "echo" and pause often produces surprising results: the rep who hears the nugget of what he/she just said, begins to truly think about what was just said. The rep may not have meant it quite that way; will think about it; temper the statement, and explain what he/she really feels or wanted to say.

Catching the last phrase of the rep's statement and repeating it may gain you much additional important information.

"Important information . . .?"

(See, you can do it—and cause the author to expand another half page on the subject! But I won't.)

Reflective Listening

As you listen to your senior rep talk (let's call him "Joe"), you sense a feeling of unfulfilled expectations. For the second time in five minutes he mentions his tenure as a sales rep: "I've been on this territory nearly three years."

"Three years?

"Well, just a little over two. But I feel like I'm getting kind of rusty.

"I guess we all get down once in a while, Joe. You seem to feel like you're in a rut, is that about it?

"Oh, sort of. My first manager kind of indicated during the interview that I'd only be on a small territory a short while.

"Hmmm. Must be frustrating, what with me coming in as your new manager and the job not being quite what you expected. Suppose you tell me about it, Joe. I wish I'd asked about your aspirations sooner."

Reflective listening is the technique of attempting to feed back to the complaining party what their feelings seem to be to check whether you understand them correctly. You mirror back what they seem to be feeling and ask for clarification or if you understand them right. Everyone wants to be understood. Yet, you cannot assume that you really understand someone else's feelings until you discuss those feelings with that person.

For example:

Then you seem to feel that (express it), is that about it? Am I reading you right? Well, if I were in your shoes, I'd probably feel the same way.

You express the reps feelings in your words to see if that is how she/he feels (doing so in an open, questioning manner) and waiting for the rep to correct your version as the rep sees fit.

Or, brief *reflective comments* may help, like, "That must be frustrating!"

Summarizing

Occasional "sum-ups" by the manager during a long discussion are helpful to both manager and sales rep. And each contact is made productive by getting some kind of agreement, to summarize what's been said, and what should be done next:

I understand better how you feel, and I'm certainly glad we had this talk. Can we agree to _____ from now on?

Even when no agreement has been reached in a conversation, it is progress to get agreement on what are the disagreements. Summarize what you have both said. Encourage the rep to suggest the next step or course of action.

All of these listening tools: Empathy, Neutrality, Proof, Clarifying, Restatement, Reflective and Summarizing—together with the questioning tools of Constructive, Fact-finding, Justifying, Return, Hypothetical, Alternative and Summarizing are handy for your skillful use and craftmanship. Use them wisely to build your people.

MOTIVATIONAL TIPS

Two-way communication motivates because it demonstrates your respect for your reps and makes them feel you are working together. To be more specific, try implementing the following:

1. Concentrate your attention on your reps' feelings and opinions. Maintain eye contact and don't interrupt.
2. Elicit opinions before giving yours.
3. Avoid asking questions that call for only "Yes" or "No" responses. Ask reflective questions which begin with, "How do you feel about . . .?" "What's your opinion on . . .?" "How would you improve . . .?"
4. Keep them informed about company developments, especially changes which will directly affect them.

Listen carefully. Not only will you obtain useful information, but you will also convey your concern and respect for the rep. This, too, earns commitment.

CHECKLIST

_____ Do you know the aspirations, ambitions, and motivations of each sales representative?
_____ For the most part, have you successfully avoided communication breakdowns?

_____ Can you honestly say that you use two-way communication with all of your sales staff?

_____ When discussing a problem with your people, do you channel the flow of discussion logically through the steps of problem solving?

_____ Do you use all appropriate Questioning and Listening tools when communicating with your staff?

_____ Do you concentrate your attention on your reps' feelings and opinions?

Chapter Ten

How to Conduct Effective Sales Meetings

Each time you gather your sales staff together for a meeting, does the investment made (in manager's/rep's time) boost sales—or depress sales? Meetings can be tremendous time savers—or tremendous time wasters. A good meeting builds morale; a bad meeting can crush morale. "Boost" or "bust," the results are determined by the group-skills of the manager. How well you design, plan, and conduct meetings that move your group to solutions/knowledge/ skills/commitment, through participation, impacts your sales team's success in the marketplace.

Lack of participation spoils meetings. Why don't all sales representatives speak out at a meeting? Why do some individuals (often the ones who could contribute most) clam up in your meeting; but talk freely about sales ideas with other reps during the break and after the meeting? Once again, your own experience can point to ways you can improve as manager: What inhibits you from speaking out at meetings with your upper management? Or with just your boss? A bit of reflection on how productive (or unproductive) were past meetings you've experienced—and what *caused* that result—may teach you a lot about how to conduct more effective meetings. Identify the fears of participants and you will know which leadership techniques best overcome them.

Aside from experience, where can you get the help you need to develop your group-skills?

This chapter will show you how to use some of the most effective, proven methods and techniques for conducting meetings aimed at solutions, knowledge, skills, and commitment such as:

- Target questions and group discussion skills.
- Bedlam practice.

- Circular idea swap.
- The grinder.
- Buzz-group discussion.
- Priorities voting.
- Round-robin of experts (Learner Controlled Instruction).
- Brainstorming.
- Cases and problems.
- Organizing an agenda.

How to get participation in sales meetings, a NSSTE Sales Success Booklet will give you additional help on the whole process of conducting sales meetings. (Write for a copy from NSSTE Headquarters, 203 E. Third St., Sanford, FL 32771-1803.)

Courses and speaking clubs, such as Dale Carnegie, Toastmasters, and the NSSTE Sales Manager Workshops give excellent instruction and opportunities to practice your group communication skills. The point is that to learn to better manage groups, you must try out these proven meeting techniques and practice, practice, practice!

HOW TO USE THE SALES MEETING FOR EFFECTIVE TRAINING

When was the first sales meeting? We're not quite sure, but it could have been when Eve and the serpent sat down in the Garden of Eden and mapped out ways to get Adam's attention, arouse his interest, create his desire for an apple, and develop the strategy for getting him to take action. Unfortunately for us, the sales meeting was a success—they closed the sale.

Ever since selling became a science that calls for planning, training, and mental conditioning, the sales meeting has been accepted as an important management tool for accomplishing those objectives. The ability to hold an effective sales meeting has become an important measurement of sales managers at any level.

Meetings offer you an excellent opportunity to accomplish group coaching. *Group coaching* is an efficient way to improve the performance level of many sales representatives at the same time. It supplements your day-to-day coaching efforts with individuals, as well as your formal (periodic) coaching of individuals. By coaching in a group, you give information and training on commonly needed skills to all your salespeople. The key to success is getting the participation of your salespeople. Getting that participation is easy as pointed out by Rodger Davenport in the NSSTE book, *The Sales Manager As A Trainer:*

> "Salespeople instinctively know that to succeed they must have information and skills. That's why so often if you just provide the basic information they need—a few ideas, a chance—that's all that's necessary. Salespeople will go the mile; just give them an inch. When they get together they generate ideas among themselves. You'll probably discover that their knowledge and skills, collectively, overwhelm yours. This fact need not threaten your security as a sales manager; it should please you, because it actually *strengthens* your position."

You, too, will learn from each group sales meeting you conduct.

WHY HOLD A MEETING?

Since planning and conducting sales meetings demands your time and effort and takes your sales reps off their sales territories, why consider meetings worth the effort? Here are a few reasons:

1. *To improve communications.* Modern business calls for better communications between you and your selling team. Salespeople don't consider themselves part of the team when they have to hear everything through the grapevine.

2. *To introduce new products or policies.* A meeting attaches more importance to the new policy or product, permits preselling practice, exchange of ideas, and prevents misunderstandings.

3. *To motivate the sales staff.* Motivation is a vital ingredient in any sales plan. Esprit de corps builds from good meetings.

4. *To solve problems.* The sales meeting makes it possible to call together those involved in the problem and those who can contribute to the solutions.

5. *To instruct and train.* The major benefit of a sales meeting is the opportunity it provides for group instruction and development. It allows you to use training techniques that are not possible on an individual basis: Bedlam Practice, Idea Exchanges, Grinders, Buzz Groups, Cases and Problems, and Brainstorming.

All five reasons given for holding sales meetings could be considered as one basic purpose—to instruct and develop salespeople. So let's look at ways in which you can use the sales meeting more effectively for that purpose.

The Sales Meeting—A Group Sale

While sales meetings vary in their mechanical details, they all have a common purpose—to *sell* the salespeople on an idea, policy, or procedure, and to get them to take enthusiastic action. Planning a sales meeting, therefore, can be approached in much the same way a professional salesperson plans an important sales presentation.

Think of your favorite formula for selling. Wouldn't it work equally well in planning a good sales meeting? Let's take the most universal and simple formula—AIDA (Attention, Interest, Desire, Action). Here's how it might function in planning a meeting.

1. *Get attention.* How you start the meeting sets the mental attitude toward the rest of the meeting.
2. *Arouse interest.* Say or do something to show how the salespeople will personally benefit by what you are going to do in the next few minutes.
3. *Create desire.* Here is your plan, your presentation, or demonstration. Like any sales, the key is convincing the salespeople of the benefits.
4. *Get action.* Too many meeting leaders stop short of this important step—closing the "sale." They consider that they have accomplished the meeting objective when they have explained a product and demonstrated its features.

In selling a product to customers, you would show how the product features result in personal benefits for them. In a sales meeting, you show how features of the meeting result in benefits for the salespeople—ways to increase sales, to sell more easily, to beat competition, to get fewer customer problems, to improve the salesperson's image with customers. You suggest a plan to the salespeople for converting the features into these benefits, and then get a commitment that they will put the new information and ideas into action.

Step One: Set the Meeting Objective

If you agree that a sales meeting is a "group sale," your first step in planning the meeting is to determine what it is you want to "sell." If you had unlimited time and a belief that the sales meeting could solve all your salespeople's problems, you might try to handle all of them at one meeting. But since you have only a few minutes, you will need to select the objectives that can be accomplished with reasonable success with a sales meeting and within the time allowed.

Limit topics.   The list of specific objectives for sales meetings can go into the hundreds. It is easy to end up with an all-purpose meeting that tries to cover too much. When this happens, the salespeople come away loaded with information but without a plan for putting anything to use. It is better to single out just those objectives that can be successfully handled by your sales formula within the time allowed.

Avoid routine.   Do not hold a sales meeting just because it is company policy to hold one every Tuesday morning from 7:30 to 8:30. When that happens, the manager often tries the night before (or at 7:00 A.M. that morning) to come up with something to fill those 60 minutes. In the same category are the sales meetings that are called because the boss says: "We gotta problem. Call a meeting for tomorrow morning." Sales meetings are costly in time and salaries for managers and sales force alike. Attending should be only those individuals who are involved in, affected by, or can contribute to the topic. If another method of communication or education would be better than a meeting, use it!

Set the specific objectives. The basic objectives of every sales meeting are to:

1. Inform.
2. Instruct.
3. Enthuse.
4. Sell.

It would be difficult to think of any sales meeting that was not intended to accomplish these four goals. More specific objectives are normally considered, however, like:

- To inform and instruct on a new product or service.
- To stimulate greater sales effort on an old product or line.
- To present a plan for getting more sales.
- To uncover problems the sales force might be having.
- To change an attitude on a product, policy, or procedure.
- To give practice and correction in selling a product, building skills of all sales reps.
- To uncover, from all the reps, the most successful techniques and ways to sell a product; and then—through practice and reciprocal coaching—improve the skill of all reps in using those techniques.

Step Two: Choose the Most Effective Group Methods

After you have established the objectives for your sales meeting, select the methods for accomplishing these objectives through group training.

Too many times, meetings involve only one-way communication. Information can be presented to the salespeople by lecture, a panel of experts, charts, dramatizations, or audiovisual aids. That information might just as easily (and less costly) be given by mail, fax, telephone, voice mail, electronic transmission, or audio or videotapes. Training, like selling, requires showing, telling, and doing: practicing and participation by the salesperson with a need for coaching and critiquing of the practice. And many times there is a need for the salespeople to work out the answers to selling problems and share experience of the group.

A different approach. Try this at your next sales meeting: Suppose . . ., just suppose . . ., that; instead of using your next district meeting to *reveal* all the information about the new (product, promotion, line, action, policy, or procedure); you get that information to your sales reps *ahead of the meeting* with instructions to come prepared to discuss and demonstrate selling it? Consider how much more productive your meeting time could be!

TARGET QUESTIONS AND GROUP DISCUSSION SKILLS

Your mastery of the seven tools of Questioning and the seven tools of Listening (from Chapter 9) need little adjustment to make you highly effective as a group discussion leader. Preplanning good target questions is essential! Because each question you ask in a group setting will influence many minds at the same time, there are certain characteristics you must build into the target (group focusing) question:

1. Singular, Selective: calls for your *best* at the moment or *one* answer. This causes each rep to focus memory on a quality response.
2. Personal: has *You* appeal, asks: "What is *your* . . .?" "What do *you* . . .?"
3. Constructive: asks for *improvement* rather than for "What's wrong?"
4. Clear, yet Brief: the meaning is crystal clear, but briefly worded.
5. Involving: commits the answerer to some form of implementation: ". . . that would command your best interest and action?" (Not what *others* should do.)
6. Attainable: within the resources (time and knowledge) of all participants, *can* be answered: "in your *opinion*," "in your *experience*."

Here are some samples of good Target Questions for meetings:

To get acquainted:

What one experience in your work might be most interesting to this group?

What one thing has happened to you since our last district meeting that you feel this group would enjoy hearing about?

What do you personally find most rewarding about your job?

To build an agenda or make a program:

If but one item of business could be handled while we are together, what would be your first choice?

What one problem concerning your work with the organization would you most like to have discussed?

What one suggestion do you have for inclusion in our next agenda which: (a) would insure your attendance and, in your opinion, the attendance of others?" or (b) would cause you to look forward to our next district meeting?

What one subject, if included in future programs, would be so meaningful to you that you would give up almost anything else to be present?

To raise questions or ideas before or after a scheduled presentation by speaker or panel:

Before: Brand manager _____ is to be our speaker. His subject will be to . . .; His qualifications and experience are . . .. To help him prepare for his presentation, what specific phase of this subject would interest you most?

After: What one question would you most like to ask in order to round out your information on this subject?"; "What additional suggestion would you offer which might contribute to the group?

To exchange experiences:

What one experience along the line of this topic would you offer which you feel would be most helpful to the group?

What additional fact can you add to help us round out your information about his subject?

What one presentation idea have you used successfully that you think could most help other sales representatives?

What is the best method (technique, activity, approach, idea, benefit) that you have used or heard about?

To canvas attitudes and to evaluate:

What, in your opinion, was the best sales accomplishment of the year?

What is your best suggestion for making the sales job (or these meetings, or activity) more purposeful and productive for you?

In what one way might we best improve district results?

In what one way do you feel this particular operation (presentation, program, policy) might be improved?

In what one way do you believe headquarters could serve you better?

What do you feel is the primary cause of the problem?

What one thing can you suggest as a solution?

What do you feel would be a positive consequence of that action?

What do you feel would be the major negative consequence?

Looking at the entire problem and all possibilities, what one action are you now willing to commit yourself to?

To motivate thinking on what has been covered:

What, in your opinion, is the greatest implication of today's meeting (material covered thus far, and so on) in terms of your job?

To get action:

In view of the discussion, what specific action should we now take that:
a. Would be so meaningful to you that you would be willing to give part of your time to it? or
b. Would command your best interest and action?

If our sales unit could adopt but one activity for company betterment, what suggestion would be so meaningful that you would pledge a part of yourself to bring it about?

What one action are you now going to take in your territory as a result of our discussion?

FIGURE 10–1

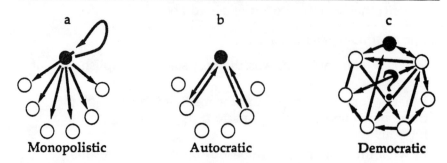

a	b	c
Monopolistic	Autocratic	Democratic

To improve relationships:

In your opinion, what should be our first step to make us a better working unit (team, staff)?

What is your best suggestion at the moment for improving our relationships within the district?

Let Your Sales Reps Do the Talking

Are you one of those sales managers who shower your staff with pearls of wisdom? Or do you treat the participants in your sales meetings as adults? If your answer to the latter question is "yes," then you know it's more important for trainees to tell you their needs, successes, and ideas than for you to lecture them about your own concerns.

Watching groups in discussion is somewhat like watching groups gather around different coaches, each with a beach ball (a specific objective). In Figure 10–1 (a), we see the monopolistic leader (the sales manager who brought the ball and likes to hog it) keep tossing it up and catching it himself as he lectures his group of assembled sales reps. His communication is all one-way, telling. He never gives the ball to anyone else. Result: Would-be players get bored, drift off, find another "ball" and start a game of their own. Down the beach at Figure 10–1 (b), the autocratic leader who brought the ball (and, therefore, makes the rules: "when I throw it to you, throw it back to me") is deliberately dealing with each rep, in turn, one-on-one. This autocratic manager controls discussion; all ideas must channel through him. He'll decide if and to whom an idea is passed on. Result: Apathy and competition for the manager's attention. Sharing of ideas between reps is minimal. It is clear that *only he* knows, it's *his* goals, *his* way, *his* brain child. But, all the noise and enthusiasm comes from up the beach where, at Figure 10–1 (c), the democratic leader has tossed up the ball to his group, making sure everyone is included in the game. The only rules: have fun and be sure everyone shares ideas. Result: Ideas bounce all around the group. Everyone learns from everyone else. Even the leader.

The best way to encourage this full participation is to use a good target question (to get discussion going) and skillfully guide discussion: you ask a target question and follow it with the word, "Anyone?"; then lead discussion by even-handed reception of responses and skilled channeling of follow-up questions.

Channeling Questions

Overhead. The overhead channel is to address the question to the entire staff by stating: "Anyone???" Wait. Someone in the group is bound to answer.

Direct. A direct channel is addressed to a specific person, but is always preceded by the name of the individual before stating the question: "Joan has several customers like we are talking about; Joan, in your opinion what is one way a sales rep can approach this 'content expert'?"

Relay. When a salesperson directs a question at you (example): ". . . and that's the way I'd approach the expert; but boss, I'd like to know other ways. Can you suggest one?" You answer: "Joan asks about other ways. How about the rest of you; what other way might you suggest to Joan?, *anyone?*" (overhead relay).

Or (direct relay): "Thanks, Joan; perhaps Al has a thought on that. Can you think of another approach to the content expert customer, Al?"

Or *Return.* You can return the question asked directly back: "Interesting you should want alternatives, Joan; can *you* think of another approach that you haven't yet tried, Joan?"

A few more suggestions on discussion leadership:

- Your role is to facilitate the discussion flow, from analysis to definition to possible actions to commitment of action plan. Be alert to those who have not spoken and look for ways to involve them. Your line of questioning and active listening (summarizing, and so on) accomplishes this.
- You cannot be both "expert" and "facilitator" at the same time, so when you interject some advice, make clear your temporary role: "Let me add something from my selling experience . . .; now, I reopen discussion to everyone. Who's next?" (You may want to have a rep lead discussion so you can concentrate on another role, such as taking notes to use in summarizing the discussion or being a resource on call by the discussion leader.)
- "Thank" every contributor and be careful not to evaluate responses. Saying "That's a great idea!" to one sales rep's response may kill subsequent ideas almost as surely as will a "put down" of a poor response. Be even-handed and respect everyone's ideas.
- Keep the discussion moving. When a "talker" monopolizes the meeting or gets off the subject, wait for them to take a breath and step in with a relay channel question that passes the ball to others in the group: "Thanks, Joe; now, can anyone else suggest how we might solve the problem of . . .?" Always control discussion for the common good but embarrass no one.
- Summarize.

BEDLAM PRACTICE

Want results? Create bedlam and let everyone practice at once!

Sales managers, in search of ways to get participation in meetings, have been advised to have participants "role play" a sales presentation. But role play, like manipulation, became (in training) a dirty word. It got that way because we trainers coerced volunteers to take a hot seat in front of a group and demonstrate how to sell. Or we put them on camera and videotaped them for later review. If you were the sales rep selected for role play, would you like it? Probably not! Before you use role play (in that fashion) in your meetings, consider that:

- It's a threatening experience.
- It's a waste of time. Only one person at a time practices when one camera is available for recording.
- It's artificial. It often uses a ficticious situation when your salespeople could be practicing for their real sales situations.

At The Dial Corporation, sales reps don't role play. They just practice and critique, practice and critique, practice and critique. Because everyone is involved in practice at the same time, they call it *bedlam practice*. It is simple. With all triads (buyer, sales rep, and observer) practicing at the same time, the noise level goes up. And so does the learning curve.

Conducting a Bedlam Session

To conduct a bedlam session, follow these five steps:

1. *Fix up a big enough place to move triads apart, yet in sight.* You can operate bedlam in the regular meeting room if there is just a little extra space for the triads to spread out from each other. They need five or six feet of space between groups in order to hear within groups. Plan ahead of time and set it up so participants can move right into the chairs for buyer, sales rep, and observer. If you are recording, have microphones and camera(s) positioned.

2. *Prepare sales situations on separate assignment sheets and have copies ready for distribution.* If you've done your homework, you had each sales rep prepare his/her own typical "selling situation," describing their "most difficult buyer." Triads use this information to prepare each buyer for practice.

3. *Break the group into teams of three for simultaneous role plays.* When assigning the three roles of sales rep, buyer, and observer, try to scatter veterans among the triads. A quick count-off is a good way to come up with new triads.

4. *Use a simplified observer-critique sheet and brief everyone on the observer's role:*
   [To take notes, to evaluate the presentation, and to critique it within the triad, pointing out "Things handled especially well," "Why the observer says so," "Suggestions for next time" regarding: the opener, the presentation, involvement of the buyer, use of visuals/samples, and the close.]

Stress the importance of good, honest feed-back to the sales rep and point out that the observer is a nonparticipant during the presentation itself; to use key words and short phrases in note-taking to help the observer's recall when critiquing the presentation.

5. *Bring on the sales reps and start bedlam practice.* Have your sales reps begin selling whenever they are ready. They should be encouraged to make the sale in a set time limit—say 15 minutes, depending on normal appointment time for buyers in your industry. When the rep completes the presentation, the triad then conducts a thorough critique led by the observer. Then they rotate roles, and the second sales rep practices his/her sales presentation.

Before you discard bedlam technique, let me counter some possible objections.

Misconception 1: It's too noisy for triads to hear. Never, in more than a thousand practices, has a single participant complained about the noise, whether in our crowded mock store or in the meeting room. Every participant has said noise was no problem. Actually, it closely approximates the background noise a sales rep encounters in real selling, in stores, the shop, or an office. You do need a slightly oversized meeting room, or room and break-out areas, where the triads can move away from other triads. Four or five feet between groups is sufficient.

Misconception 2: It applies only to sales presentations. Not so. Bedlam practice improves skills of all kinds: demonstrating, presenting, interviewing, answering objections, dealing with irate customers, teaching, communication, listening, practicing manual operations, or anything involving practice of a skill.

Misconception 3: You need many trainers to be effective. Wrong again! You will find that your sales reps will be better critiquers and teachers of each other than are outside trainers. I've used it *alone* with more than 150 manager trainees in one ballroom. There is no reason why you, the manager, should not join in on the fun as part of a triad. You will learn, too. Fact is that you will have to shift your concept from being God—the critiquer—to one of facilitating the real teachers—the sales reps themselves—so they learn a maximum from each other.

Misconception 4: You can't use videotaping with bedlam. Bedlam was used for years before video came along, and bedlam practice works better without it. Video recording can scan all groups practicing at the same time and catch excerpts from the practice. These excerpts can be used as discussion starters after the bedlam session is over. Today's tiny camcorders left unattended on tripods about the practice area are hardly noticed by sales reps during practice.

CIRCULAR IDEA SWAP

Have you observed during discussion in meetings, the person with the most information often holds back while the less informeds dominate? It happens more than it should. There are also many occassions where it would help to hear the experiences or opinions of every member of your staff: as an icebreaker (by having each member give a 60 second speech about themselves); as a sampling (of the problems the reps are encountering on their territories); as a swapping of know-how or ideas (tell and show of the very best in each rep's experience); for compiling a list (of causes, or possible solutions, or actions to be taken); and for getting commitment (by asking "What one action are you going to take back on the job as a result of our discussion here?").

At your next meeting, why not go around the room with discussion using the circular response method?

Rules of the Game

Here are suggestions for a successful circular idea swap:

1. Prepare a clear, brief, single target question.
2. Arrange chairs in a circle when possible (if more than fourteen, two circles).
3. Announce the rules of the game and decide on a time limit for each contribution. (Frequently, one minute is the time agreed upon.)
4. Be sure each member understands the question. Then allow one or two minutes for each member to write out his/her own response. Call time, then allow one minute more for each member to reduce his response to the briefest possible number of words. (This is to assist the recorder or the chalkboard operator.) However, advise that each salesperson will have his/her full minute to expand on the brief statement.

5. Start with a volunteer, then call on each member in turn, clockwise or counter-clockwise, until each has had his/her chance.
6. Each person has the privilege of:
   a. Responding within the time limit agreed upon.
      1) Bringing new ideas or combining and improving on ideas already given.
      2) Commenting upon previous answers.
   b. Passing.
   c. Asking that his/her minute be spent in silence "so everyone may think more deeply."
7. There can be no interruptions and no speaking out of turn. Upon concluding each round, invite those who "passed" to add their comments if they wish.
8. The number of times around the circle will depend on many factors:
   a. The group's belief that the subject has been explored enough.
   b. The frequency of those who pass up the opportunity to speak.
   c. Time limits for the discussion.
9. Careful recording of all comments should provide adequate background for arriving at some general conclusions or discussion leading to action.

Circular response is especially useful in discussions involving controversy or where you want to get many ideas on the table prior to general discussion. It is also excellent for getting individual commitments to action at the conclusion of a meeting.

THE GRINDER

The grinder is a group participative process that seems to produce more improvement in the skill of participants, faster than any other training process. It allows simultaneous practice by half your trainees for a set, time sequence; then instant feedback critique with specific suggestions to improve; followed by tryout on a new and different buyer with his/her critique and further, additional practice on third and subsequent buyers.

Organizing the Grinder

Here's how to orchestrate the grinder:

1. Have everyone prepare a sales presentation complete with visuals.
2. Split your group into two equal parts (I have them count off, odd numbers becoming "sales reps," even, "buyers"). Have them line up one-on-one (seller and buyer) across a long table with all buyers on one side, sellers on the other.

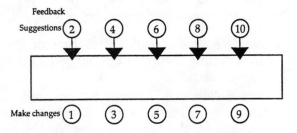

3. Announce time limits for the sellers' presentations (three minutes, or five minutes, or ten, depending on your product). Set bell timer and shout: "Begin selling!"
4. When bell rings, stop all sales presentations and announce a time limit (say two-three minutes) for each buyer to critique his or her seller. The buyer should be instructed to give at least one suggestion for improvement in the seller's presentation. Instruct sellers to add suggested changes to their material. Then start the timer again and tell buyers to "Start coaching feedback."

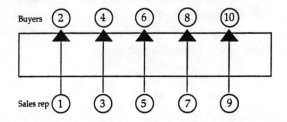

5. When bell timer rings, tell the group the sellers will now "grind" by moving to the next chair to their right (buyers stay put) and (to a new buyer) they will be making their presentations anew using the suggestions of the previous buyer.

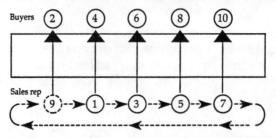

6. Sellers make presentations to at least three or four buyers in succession, getting feedback and suggestions for improvement from each.

7. Reverse roles. Sellers now become buyers, and the grind is continued. Before having the class change roles, ask buyers to cast ballots for the best presenter. At the conclusion of the two practice sessions, the winners make their presentations to the class.

You will see great improvement in a short time because feedback and tryout is immediate!

BUZZ GROUP DISCUSSION

Have you ever noticed how, at the end of a sales meeting, staff members form clusters of three or four sales reps and talk, talk, talk? People's fear of speaking out in large groups and their enthusiasm for communicating in safe, small groups can be put to work right in your staff meetings. Here's how you can use this proven technique, known as buzz group discussion (or discussion 66). Your group should be seated as shown.

Take any problem which affects your group and for which you seek the best thought of every member. Phrase this objective into a target question: specific, clear, brief, constructive, and personal. Be sure it is expressed in the language of your people, and is understood by all. Allow each individual a couple of minutes to think and write down his/her brief response.

Announce: "To let everyone share thoughts with neighbors and save time, we will get together in groups of three to five, where each group is to select a chairperson to see that every person shares his or her ideas, and a secretary will record and report back to the total group. Have I made myself clear? OK, move to your group."

When each buzz group has time to get acquainted and has decided on a chairperson and secretary, give them six minutes to discuss their answers to the target question, then give each group a few minutes to screen ideas, checking the one or two which seem most important for sharing with the total staff.

Ask: "Is there any group not ready to report?" When all groups are ready, return to original conference seating so everyone can see the chart pad (or chalkboard). Have each buzz group's secretary report these main ideas to the entire staff, screened and summarized for the benefit of all, as you add them to the pad/board.

PRIORITIES VOTING

Let's say you recorded six ideas (reported by the buzz groups' secretaries) on the chart pad. You ask: "Does any secretary-reporter have, written on their list, an idea that is different from those on my pad?" (If so, add to your list.) In our example, two more are reported and listed for a total of eight.

General discussion and review of the group's ideas is usually productive.

What should you do with the ideas that are briefed on the chart pad? You can either: (a) charge each of your reps to pick one, tell how he/she plans to implement that idea on the job, and commit to doing so; or (b) test the total group's concensus.

True concensus can be arrived at by having each member of your team vote for more than one of the items listed, using this process and by following the example shown:

1. On the chart pad, number consecutively the items listed, in this example, from one to eight.

2. Ask the group to: "Look over the list and pick those items, two or three of them, that you strongly agree with. Write down on a piece of paper the numbers corresponding to items you vote for. Pick more than one." (Multiple votes solves being torn between choices of several good ideas; one doesn't have to throw out the baby with the bath water.)

3. Ask: "By show of hands, how many wrote down the digit one?, two, three, . . .?" (Getting them to write down the digits that identify ideas eliminates popularity voting: that is, seeing how friends vote before commiting.)

4. Record votes on the margin of the pad. It will be clear from the votes as to the group's ranking of items.

ROUND-ROBIN OF EXPERTS

When a new product or line of new products is about to be introduced in your area, you may decide to call your sales reps to a meeting. Often, a delegation of product specialists from company headquarters is brought into such a meeting to assist with training on the new product(s). To prepare your sales team to be

FIGURE 10–2

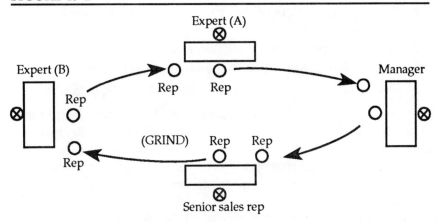

the best at selling the new line, use the help of these experts beyond mere input of product knowledge: have the experts help your sales reps prepare and make sales presentations on the new products. After basic information is given to all sales representatives, have each rep develop a specific sales presentation with help from one product expert; then put reps through grinder practice as shown in Figure 10–2 with the experts and management as buyers.

Have each "expert" sit at a table (as a consultant) with all available product information, samples, brochures. Set two or three chairs opposite the consultants for help-seeking sales representatives.

For a set time period, sales reps seek out the consultant of choice who helps the rep with development of a personalized sales presentation. (This is Learner-Controlled Instruction.)

When time period for preparation expires, begin grinder practice with experts, managers, and your most senior sales reps as buyers.

BRAINSTORMING

Creativity is greatest when people act together. The brainstorming session takes advantage of this fact, using the ideas of one salesperson to spark the thoughts in another. Competition increases the group's accomplishment. Brainstorming is a method used within problem solving and consists of separation of the idea getting stage from the other steps of problem solving. This temporary separation allows you to use new rules of discussion:

1. *Quantity* of ideas count—not quality.
2. *All* ideas are welcome, tell them as quickly as they come to mind.
3. There is to be *no critical judgment.*
4. Wildness of ideas counts—*any* idea is acceptable.
5. Idea-hitchhiking is encouraged—*build on* the ideas of others.

These rules apply during the idea getting phase. Your desire for a *lot* of ideas must be made known. Show enthusiasm. Record the ideas quickly; this may require two or more people to write alternately on several chart pads as quickly as ideas are expressed. Your staff will come up with many dozens of ideas in only four or five minutes.

The other phases of the problem solving process require judgment and considerably more time. If five minutes are allowed for idea getting, approximately 15 minutes to a half-hour should be allowed the group for: *Idea-sorting* (Examine all ideas, even wild ones, for a clue to something sound. Sort sound from unsound, eliminating futile ideas); *Idea-weighing* (discuss the most workable ideas and analyze the pros and cons of each idea); *Idea-implementing* (those few ideas the group feels are worth implementing are developed into plans).

Brainstorming is especially good on problems dealing with new ventures or for snapping reps out of too traditional thinking. Like: closing those accounts that never seem to buy; developing a locally originated promotion; solving a problem that has frustrated previous efforts. A "gem" of an idea may surface.

CASES AND PROBLEMS

The case method and problem solving are techniques used with the conference, seminar, or workshop method of group training. The case or problem forms the topic on which the discussion is based. The case or problem may be an actual or hypothetical one. In our experience, it is far better to use the actual cases or problems of the sales reps attending than to use a hypothetical case.

A case study is a story or a problem plus solutions attempted so far. The group considers the facts, identifies the primary causes, defines the key question, evaluates solutions, and recommends conclusion(s). By using actual cases of participants, you help the owner of each problem toward a better resolution of his or her problem and others learn from sharing ideas that solve real sales problems.

ORGANIZING AN AGENDA

Where do most meetings go wrong? From our observation, the *three weak areas* are: failure to build readiness, not identifying problem causes and failure to wrap up. Sales managers who run the most successful meetings are able to move the group through five steps of group process: 1. Building *readiness;* 2. Expose the *Problem;* 3. Explore *causes;* 4. Evaluate *ideas;* and 5. *Wrap-up.* All the while, the leader must keep in mind the objectives of the meeting participants to assure win-win results.

Build the readiness of the participants. This starts in advance of the meeting, with your invitation or notice to attend that lists: time and place, expected duration, purpose of the meeting, agenda, materials to bring, and request to come prepared to contribute ideas on what subjects. Preplan. What is your priority problem; background; why a problem? Frame the target question to be presented. Plan the sizzle: how and why your reps are involved, why they should spend their time on this subject, benefits (to the company and to them) that can come from fruitful discussion. At your meeting: have the room arrangements preset for ease of discussion, greet reps at the door, build readiness by a brief get acquainted, and sell them that this is worth their time and thought. Express the need for their best thinking and ideas.

Expose the problem. Set the stage for discussion: describe the situation. Just facts, no blame and no suggestions at this stage, simply the conditions that exist. Point out losses that the reps have a stake in and *question* them about these losses (to get agreement that these losses are important to them).

Explore causes. Tap your sales reps' experience, observations, opinions, and knowledge to uncover all possible causes of the problem. Use discussion techniques that aid identifying the real causes of your priority problem. Sum up what seems to be the main cause and pose a question of solutions.

Evaluate ideas. Tap your staff members' ideas and suggestions for solutions. Uncover a number of possible actions. Get your group to analyze the possibilities and share opinions of advantages and disadvantages of each possible action. Survey for consensus.

Repeat the problem solving sequence of these past three steps with every problem you've selected as an objective of your meeting, as time allows. Do not attempt too much; it is better to deal well with two or three priority objectives than to touch lightly and inconclusively on a dozen or more.

Wrap-up. This is the most important step of all: getting commitment of every sales rep to take some follow-up action as a result of the group discussion! Sum up your meeting with the benefits of taking the right actions and conduct an "alter call": WHAT will be done? WHO will do it? WHEN it will be done? Circular idea swap is a good way to get individual commitments: ask; "What actions are you now going to take in your job to implement at least one of the ideas resulting from this meeting?" Some managers give the reps a few minutes to write down their responses, then collect the paper commitments for later follow through. You can have each rep state his/her planned actions to the group. Tell how you intend to use the ideas expressed at the meeting and how you will proceed. Express your appreciation for the sales reps' participation and ideas. Close the meeting.

CHECKLIST

_____ Do your meetings more than pay for themselves in terms of sales results versus all the costs?

_____ Do you carefully preplan each meeting to deal with only those objectives that can be accomplished with reasonable success within the time allowed?

_____ Are questions you use to focus discussion *singular, personal, constructive, clear and brief, involving, and attainable*?

_____ Is there at least one participative technique listed in this chapter that you now intend to use in your next staff meeting?

_____ Are you satisfied that your skills of channeling discussion through questions gets the thought process of your group to the objective effectively without leaving anyone out?

_____ Do your staff meetings move members to solutions, knowledge, skills, and commitment through participation?

Chapter Eleven

How to Evaluate Team Members' Performance

All the How-to's offered in this book come together in the Goal Discussion Process described in this chapter. Apply your skills to this process and you will develop the best sales team possible! But, like any tool, its results depend on how skillfully you use it. The professional manager uses goal discussions to fine-tune performance and accelerate development; the unskilled manager may actually diminish performance and inhibit development by misusing, or not using, performance appraisals.

FOCUS AHEAD, NOT BEHIND!

Troubles arise when some managers do "appraisals" because their evaluations of sales reps are perceived by the reps as judgmental nit-picking exercises rather than helpful results oriented coaching on business planning. We advocate a process in which you, the sales manager, conduct periodic goal setting discussions with each of your sales representatives to: (1) objectively review recent achievement of results toward the previously agreed to goals, (2) identify job areas of difficulty, (3) explore the reasons for difficulty and ways to overcome difficulties, (4) establish new goals and develop a workable plan of action for accomplishing those goals—doing so in a way that leads to corporate and personal growth. This process requires both a discussion and a document that summarizes your best coaching assistance and motivates the sales rep to self-development and self-management. With the document (a written plan-of-action summary of the goal discussion), each sales rep can manage and develop to the maximum without close supervision.

In Chapter two, "How to Set Clear Goals," we advised quarterly reviews of each sales rep's responsibilities, indicators, and goals as a way to implement self-management by objectives (SMBO). You were given a tool: a blank form; and encouraged to mutually prepare a working job description, that is, a list of responsibilities, indicators of performance, and goals (or standards of performance) with each of your sales representatives. If you followed through, you and the sales representative now have a list of the specific standards of performance, or goals, for that sales person. The list of responsibilities, indicators, and goals describes specifically what results you expect, that is; what the job will look like when "well done." The initial, joint development of a goals list, with a copy retained by each rep, provides your sales reps with a tool by which they can largely manage themselves. This relieves you of the need to give constant, close supervision. You now have more time to manage proactively; plan and develop your district's business; teach, coach, coordinate, and build your top performing sales team.

Why Isn't Informal, Day-to-Day Coaching Enough?

On week-to-week contacts with each member of your team, and your occasional ride withs, you focus on specific needs of the individual, solve immediate problems and accomplish tactical coaching. During these contacts, you are continuously appraising the performance of your subordinates and providing feedback of what you see.

The need for periodic or "formal" coaching. Each of your sales reps wants to know "how am I doing over-all?" Because you deal with *immediate* problems in daily supervision, over time each sales representative may get a distorted view of his/her overall needs. Regular, periodic, eyeball to eyeball discussions are necessary to develop a realistic understanding of *all* parts of the sales job; to know exactly what progress has been made and why; to reset goals for the upcoming period of time and develop necessary plans for meeting those goals. These strategic or periodic reviews are often called: "appraisal interviews"; the process of "annual coaching"; human "preventive maintenance check-ups." This formal meeting of the minds to refocus the sales rep on his or her total job is necessary because you have naturally shown concern in day-to-day contacts on immediate problems. Chances are that, over six months of normal contact, some responsibilities of the sales representative have never been reviewed or discussed with the individual.

How often do you review overall performance? Strategic coaching is *planned*. It is longer range than the informal, day-to-day coaching that takes place on the job. You need to supplement and assist day-to-day coaching by setting up plans for job performance, training, and development. It is a joint, problem-solving discussion (of the total job) between manager and sales rep. The fast pace of today's sales job requires reviews far more frequent than annually. You will probably find it best to review goals quarterly. Some sales managers bring their sales teams together and use group process skills to get shared reports of progress and plan the accomplishment of individual and team goals. These quarterly discussions to review progress on goals and assist with the sales representative's business planning can be alternated with expanded, individual, performance appraisal discussions at semi-annual and annual intervals.

THE GOAL DISCUSSION PROCESS

A well executed Goal Discussion sets new goals and plans for achieving those goals. To remove difficulties to future performance, you will have to look back, learn from difficulties in past performance, and get answers to four questions:

1. "What results did we get this past quarter in your territory?"
2. "Why did we get these results?"
3. "What can we learn from it to help get better results next quarter?"
4. "Specifically, what *will* we do?"

Two Mistakes to Avoid

The strong developmental value of the process of periodic goal setting is stifled if an appraisal document is created:

1. Without employee input.
2. With intent to justify an already decided personnel action, that is; promote, demote, pay change or to otherwise build a case. In managing the sales representatives on your payroll, you are periodically expected to do two kinds of review: performance enhancement, and compensation. *They must not be mixed!* These two discussions must be separated in time. A performance enhancement discussion is training. A salary review discussion is personnel administration. (Combining contaminates the developmental process by your need to justify the prediscussion decision of planned salary action.) It is best to hold the performance enhancement discussion (Goal Discussion) at least a month *before* any regular salary review is due (and refuse to discuss compensation at that time). Then reward on results when you review compensation. The Goal Discussion Summary document is excellent evidence for that later action.

Let's look at the best process to use for a performance enhancement review.

A THREE-PHASE PROCESS

The goal discussion process reviewed here has three phases:

I. Mutual Preparation (it involves input by both employee and manager).

II. Goal Discussion Meeting (A joint five-step interview. Because you will want to cause the rep's best thought process and highest motivation toward achieving productivity goals, you need to follow a format that moves the discussion and planning process logically).

III. Goal Discussion Summary Document (the summarizing map that guides the sales rep to self-management by objectives). Figure 11-1 shows a format to use.

FIGURE 11-1
Sales Representative Goal Discussion Worksheet

INSTRUCTIONS: *Complete sections I, II, III as preparation for upcoming goal discussion. At discussion, establish plan (IV).*

Name:	Supervisor:	
Period Reviewed *From To*	*Goals Set* *From To*	*Date To Be Discussed* *Planned Actual*
I. Review all goal areas, previous goals, and results actually achieved.	**II. Probable causes** Determine probable cause of performance.	**III. New goals** proposed.

FIGURE 11-1 (concluded)

I. **Review** all goal areas, previous goals, and results actually achieved.	II. **Probable Causes** Determine probable cause of performance.	III. **New Goals** proposed.

IV. PLAN OF ACTION

Result Wanted	What Will Be Done, By Whom, To What Level?	Start Date	End Date
1. _____			
2. _____			
3. _____			
4. _____			
5. _____			

The *Goal Discussion Worksheet* is offered here as a *worksheet*. It can help you in preparation for a successful goal discussion or appraisal of performance no matter what the format of your own company's appraisal form. You can use this worksheet to guide performance enhancement efforts and, when completed, you may copy results onto your required reporting form (if it is different). Here is how the process works best.

Phase I. Mutual Preparation

Have the sales rep make a self-appraisal. It is important that the subordinate perceive the need for changing. Ask the subordinate to appraise his/her own performance against goals by considering how well he/she thinks the responsibilities were carried out and goals met. You can make it easier for the sales rep to make this self-appraisal by informing him/her a week or more in advance of your planned discussion and by giving the rep a worksheet with goals and (most) results filled in. Here's how:

1. Using the format of Figure 11–1, the GDS Worksheet, review all goal areas (responsibilities) and specific goals (from the R-I-G list) against the actual results (from sales records, productivity reports, observations). When you, the sales manager, have filled the left column (I.) with all the *goals* and available data (numbers) of *actual results* (achievement information available to you), make two copies.

I. **Review** all goal areas, previous goals, and results actually achieved.	II. **Probable causes** Determine probable cause of performance.	III. **New goals** proposed.

2. Give one copy of the Worksheet showing goals and results to the sales representative. Ask the rep to do three things

in preparation for the (next week's) discussion session
with you:

a. Make a self-appraisal by reviewing results against goals.
b. To determine and write down (in section II) all probable
   causes of that performance.
c. Propose and write in (III) new goals he/she wants to commit to (believes they can achieve) in the time period ahead.

Make an appraisal of the subordinate's performance. Appraise the sales rep's performance and do your own thorough
homework *before* discussing it with him/her. Note performance
areas where the rep had difficulty or where the new goal may cause
difficulty. Write in second person singular style: "Sal, you . . .";
a helpful, coaching tone of writing.

Consider probable causes of performance results. It is
often unwise to jump straight from results achieved to new goals
without first analyzing real world causes—the WHY! "Why is it
that this responsibility is not being carried out satisfactorily? Is it
due to the sales rep? Attitude? Skill? Knowledge? If so, specifically
which one? Am I responsible? Is it other factors?" Pin down
several causes. Example:

> If a goal of selling 100 units was not achieved, will establishing a new
> goal of 110 improve performance? Probably not. However, a review of
> *causes* of performance . . . poor time management, ineffective rout-
> ing, failure to properly qualify prospects, poor call planning, not iden-
> tifying the needs of potential customers . . . allows you an opportu-
> nity for discussion, building awareness, and establishing a plan of
> action to improve performance. Perhaps to sell 115, or 150!

It is also helpful to consider the causes for satisfactory performance.
Identifying causes for goal attainment helps you build awareness
of how to get positive future sales results. Complete section II of
your copy of the form by determining the most probable causes of
performance results (both good and bad) and note these to bring
out in the discussion.

**Propose new goals and check your plan with your own
boss.** By evaluating past results and causes of those results, you
can now realistically recommend new goals you want achieved in

a specific future time period. On your worksheet, write these recommended goals in the right hand column, Section III: New Goals. These state what you plan to propose as the sales rep's new goals in each result area. Usually, it is best to review this plan for an appraisal with your own boss before the discussion with the rep. This takes advantage of one more set of eyes and may add to your insight of results, causes, and future goals; as well as providing another view of the individual needs of your team members.

Consider possible actions.   Think about possible actions that might be taken to remedy the causes.

Consider the individual and set objectives of your interview.   Establish a specific objective (what you want the sales rep to do differently as a result of the goal discussion and how you want him/her to feel when the interview is over). If the employee is thick-skinned, you can use a different approach than with one who is oversensitive.

Schedule the interview.   A private place, preferably without interruptions.

Phase II. The Goal Discussion Meeting

The goal discussion meeting is conducted using input prepared by both the manager and employee. This meeting's objective is to discuss results achieved, causes of performance, and then establish new goals with a clearly understood plan of action designed for critical development areas. A five-step pattern is evident in the most successful appraisal interviews:

(Move the Discussion Toward →)
1. Warm up→2. Evaluation→3. Causes→4. Possible actions→ 5. Plan

It starts with an introductory "warm up" step that precedes the four questions we listed earlier: "What results did we get? Why? What can we learn from that? What will we do?". Thus, the logical steps: (1) Warm up, (2) Review of results, (3) Causes, (4) Possible actions and (5) Plan of action. You will want to study these steps in detail and then apply all your managerial tools with skill to move each sales rep to commitment to his/her plan of action for accomplishing high standards of performance.

Step	*Objective of the step*
1. *Warm up.* Explain the purpose of the interview, point out mutual value to you both. Stress that it is to be a joint problem-solving session. Tell sequence you would like to follow in the interview. (Best sequence is the prioritized Responsibility list.)	Reduce tension. Set the stage.
2. *Evaluation.* Use either a direct approach (supervisor lays his "cards on the table" first), getting the subordinate's reaction to your appraisal; or an indirect (supervisor plays it cozier), getting comments and opinions from your subordinate before you commit yourself. Neither approach is necessarily "best." Pin down and get agreement on which items of performance require improvement and are worthy of further discussion in this interview.	Frank exchange of opinions. Resolve differences of opinions. Get agreement on what are difficult areas (identify problems).
3. *Causes.* Avoid skipping from "What's wrong?" directly to "What to do about it?" Spend time discussing all the underlying factors that are causing the current situation. Does the rep have sufficient basic ability? Lack motivation? Personal characteristics? Experience? How about me (the manager)? Objectives clear? Granted adequate authority? Given proper priority to the various responsibilities? Manpower? How about the situation: advertising or promotions cancelled? Technical problems? Competition? Policies or procedures account for difficulties? (Find the reasons.)	Understanding of the real causes of performance.

Step	Objective of the step
4. *Set new goals and possible actions.* Discuss and agree on new goals for the upcoming period. For "tough" goals, brainstorm possible actions. Get as many actions on the table as possible. Call for creative thinking.	Set realistic goals. Get agreement. Exploration of many actions.
5. *Plan of action.* Review possible actions. Outline *Who* is going to do *What* and *When* it's to be done. A sequence of small steps is more likely to be completed successfully than a single, long, complex action. Avoid generalities like "get better" or "work on." Put it in writing. Conclude the discussion by summarizing what has taken place (why you got together, what has taken place, what you have accomplished).	Practical plan.

Phase III. The Goal Discussion Summary Document

When you have completed phases I and II, the sales representative has a much clearer understanding of past accomplishments and a clear direction of what has to be done in the upcoming period. But memories are short, especially in the tough competitive day-to-day battle your sales reps must wage. By summarizing the mutual input of your goal discussion meeting, the goal discussion Document, in the hands of the rep, serves as a frequent reference and guide. Write up the agreed to Plan of Action and summarize your evaluation with a description of development needed. The worksheet itself can serve as the summary document, or you can use it's information on your own format. The important thing is to give the sales rep a copy.

Here are a few last-minute tips:

- Focus on the *job*, not the person.
- Set objectives with *realistic stretch.*
- Put emphasis on *realism.*
- State objectives in language that is *understandable* by both parties.

- Keep objectives *limited* in number (six to eight); resist the "laundry list."
- Utilize *known reports and data* as yardsticks.
- Establish a reasonable *timetable* as the measurement period.
- Approach each session with an open mind—*negotiate professionally.*

A CAREER DISCUSSION

What about the sales rep with good potential for a bigger job? Or the rep who wants to talk to you about promotion, whether qualified or not?

Don't dodge such a discussion; neither should you ever imply a promise about future personnel action or shut the door to future opportunities. But you can use a five-step discussion format similar to the goal discussion. The difference is focus. After determining the job aspired to, you must focus discussion on mutual understanding of the requirements of the future job (rather than results in the current job), which requirements are not currently fully met, and on efforts that can be made in the future to meet the requirements. Challenge your people to develop themselves and then provide them the skilled coaching required.

CHECKLIST

_____ As part of my day-to-day coaching, I make notes and plans anticipating the next periodic coaching interview.

_____ As part of each periodic coaching interview, my sales rep and I plan follow-up action of an informal nature.

_____ I make a conscious effort to improve upon my interviewing skills.

_____ I am making plans to conduct periodic "preventive maintenance" interviews with every one of my staff members.

_____ I have the sales representative make a self-appraisal before each Goal Discussion.

_____ A discussion of the causes of performance precedes any decision of what to do about performance.

_____ I reward according to results by seeing that financial rewards, praise, and credit goes to those reps who have produced results—without exception. My reps know and understand this.

Chapter Twelve

How to Develop Your Team Building Skills: A Summary Checklist

A friend of mine, who specializes in the nutshell approach to sales management, says, "A manager's job is to accelerate the growth of his or her people." In my book, that's solid advice.

The question then becomes, "What can you, as a sales manager, do to speed people on their way to success?" Comfortingly, if your associates make the grade in your company, you almost automatically will too.

Sales managers, like other people, learn best by doing. Individuals tend to retain, and are able to pass on, those skills and techniques that are part of their personal experience package. Not very many nonswimmers end up as water-safety instructors. Very few pure spectators at athletic events would make great college quarterbacks. Most leaders in industry or elsewhere have spent some time in apprenticeship earning their stripes in the field, on the line, or at somebody's knee. Those responsible for the development of other people need to arrange learning opportunities for their compatriots that are true to life, participative, and as individualized as possible.

As a sales manager, if you are to acquaint people with the techniques of being effective on the telephone, what better evidence is there of your resource proficiency than a demonstration, in the trainee's presence, of your telephone effectiveness? As a sales manager, if you are to school field representatives in call planning, what better way can that subject be broached than by your scheduling the geography as if it were yours? There are several peripheral points here.

1. As a manager, it's not important that you be a better telephone communicator, a better call planner, or a better account strategist than any of your salespeople. At the same time, the inability to handle these tasks at all would be unacceptable.

2. For training purposes, being able to "do" as well as to manage will build for you a world of personal confidence which the unscathed delegator will never know.

3. An ongoing personal experiment, which I've conducted with management groups for years, asks the question posed in Chapter 1,: "What are the characteristics of the best boss you've ever had—what are the things that make this person a standout in your mind?" One of the universal replies to that question has been, "The boss was a 'come on' rather than a 'go on' kind of person—showed me how—was a good operator—wasn't afraid to get in there and work." The suggestion here is that some of the success in sales management runs parallel with the selling skills you and your people share jointly.

An early suggestion then for new sales managers would be that they avail themselves of the training provided for sales personnel. By so doing, they can begin to learn what they'll eventually need to teach. Chances are, like most sales managers, you came up through the ranks of salespeople, selling. Once those selling and organizational skills are tucked away in an experience savings account, other important management devices can be mastered— and it's those that we'll deal with next.

MANAGING MUSTS FOR SALES MANAGERS

Attitude

If providing knowledge to trainees is represented by a number one on the difficulty scale, and providing skills calls for a number two on that measuring stick, then attitude development rates a number six—it's the toughest task of all. Maybe, as in other segments of business life, those training achievements that are the hardest to come by are the most important of all.

Now, how do you encourage, promote, cultivate, and develop a powerful positive attitude for your people? My answer is the climate you set. That climate is pretty well told by how you practice actions listed in the *Coaching Checklist* (at the end of this chapter), summarizing this book's guidelines. The point is this: A positive attitude is almost impossible if the climate is overly restrictive, inattentive, and uncommunicative. A good question for all of us to ask is: "What can I do to improve the managerial climate for my people?" The rest takes care of itself.

Administrative Skills

For a new sales manager, learning administrative skills is a little like tying a brand new necktie or scarf. If you get it right the first time, the folds will fall into place on each subsequent try, and you can then concentrate your attention on more important things even while the tying is taking place.

Sales administration brings to most people a flood of forms, reports, requests, directives, policies, correspondence, data transmission, and paperwork which they are not prepared to handle. The need most people have is for a mechanism and a concept that provides for the orderly disposition of the data and paper blizzard. The key here is to learn the time saving tips (from Chapter 3) early in your career as manager, long before the feeling of drowning and sinking can set in. Here are some specific suggestions:

1. Meet with your manager and have him/her go over the paperwork that is new to you. Find out the frequency and importance of forms, how to read and interpret them, and, most importantly, what paper can be thrown away and when.

2. Set up a basic system of administrative information filing, with files keyed to each individual salesperson in your district. Sort mail into priorities. After sorting, handle each piece of paper only once . . . act on it. Make "To-Do" lists. Do "A"s, not "C"s.

3. Delegate what you can and use clerical assistance fully.

Efficient sales administration keeps the decks clear for action, keeps desk time to a minimum, and keeps you from becoming entangled in the flypaper of sales documents and written communication.

Training Skills

In most companies of moderate size, training salespeople is a shared responsibility between the sales training manager and the field management team. The relationship is much like that between a school and a home in educating youngsters. When both parts of the equation function at their best, a synergism is born, and the results can be marvelous to see. Conversely, when either half of the partnership is deficient or neglectful, the impact on learning is diminished more than 50 percent.

To feel more comfortable in your all important role as the primary trainer of your people, review again the basics of how to train given in Chapter 6. Books, publications, and tapes that can help are listed in the next chapter: "Training Resources."

In addition, here are some observations on the whole process of field training that can be beneficial.

1. Training seeks a change in behavior—you want someone to do something differently. Expect progress not in leaps and bounds, but in moderate and measurable steps. We can all change, but we do that by degrees rather than quadrants.

2. We learn by *doing*, not by watching. In field training, as quickly as possible, have the salesperson carry the ball on all calls even at the risk of occasional lost orders. Salespeople operate 95 percent of the time alone. A manager's job is to train salespeople, while with them, to be productive on their own.

3. Make training trips as much a part of your quarterly schedule as reading your mail. Schedule work-withs in collaboration with your salespeople and agree in advance on the kinds of calls you want to make and on the length of your stay.

4. Set a fast pace for yourself and your people when you're working together. Have an air of urgency. Show high expectations.

5. Use positive reinforcement as a correctional device. Dwell on strengths, not weaknesses. Praise generously, and specifically.

6. Record in writing, for yourself and your salespeople, the results of your trip: what was accomplished, what is yet to be done, when progress will be made. Give the salesperson a copy.

7. Finally, with people on your probation list, let your travel observations enable and compel you to raise the question: "Will this individual be successful from his or her own perspective and for us in this job?" If not, then in the name of fairness and humaneness, set the wheels in motion to make a personnel change in that territory. Neither the sales representative, nor the company, nor you are well-served by people who are mismatched to their jobs. Do the decent thing for all three parties, and program yourself to make a change.

Recruiting

Whatever your goals may be in sales management, you can recruit your way to success. In other words, you can select and bet on the horses, even if you can't run with them. It is impossible to overstate the importance of hiring people with outstanding potential. Avoid having to train untrainables. Someone in my circle of friends says, "If you hire clods and train them, you have trained clods." What actions, then, can a sales manager take to assure a supply of candidates that ought to beat the average when measured against human mainstream initiative, performance, and potential? Besides rereading Chapter 5: "How to Select and Recruit Better Sales Team Members," we suggest the following:

1. Make sure you're involved in the recruiting and hiring process. Don't let somebody else arbitrarily pick your people for you. All of us have sets of likes and dislikes. It's much easier and more effective for us to work with people we like than it is for us to associate intimately with those that have been thrust upon us. Take the position that as sales manager, if you're responsible for sales production in a piece of geography, you'd like to participate in deciding who will work that territory.

2. Be recruiting minded. A published author that I've read says that first level sales managers can afford to spend 10 percent of their time searching for and screening sales candidates. You may question that percentage. Nonetheless, the point to be made is the desirability of keeping your personnel eyes and ears open for potential hires, and doing that on a daily basis.

A manager I know keeps a little black book with names of people he has met socially, on business calls, in airplanes, has read about, and has heard others talk about. When a territory opening is imminent, that manager has a prospect list of 50 people with whom to start; and even if none of the 50 want a job, those 50 names will lead to perhaps 50 more.

3. Maintain a very personal contact with one or two potential sources of names. That contact may be an employment firm, a college alumni bureau, a company personnel manager, or a fellow sales manager. These contacts ought to be cultivated and nourished on a regular basis, not just when the need arises.

4. Run your job finalists through as many screens as you can. It's just as important to a potential employee to locate the right opportunity as it is for the sales manager to select a square peg for a matching receptical. Have your candidate interviewed by several people in your company. Run a thorough track record check on the potential associate. Encourage all applicants to spell out their goals to see if they match yours. In short, eliminate all the guesswork you can at the front-end of the relationship, and avoid having to hire again in three months.

Motivation

Individuals in a sales force are not all alike in their needs and wants. For that reason, it is critical to deal with people on a one-on-one basis, attempting to discern, for each, what turns them on or off.

Every sales rep is an energy package. A manager's job is to get a high and sustained application of that energy in accomplishing one's business objectives.

What percentage of the available energy do you now get?

To light that energy to its maximum in your reps, you must do what fifty years of corporate North American trainers' experience suggests in this book. You will structure sales jobs that allow people in those slots to find the humanizing, rewarding kinds of stimulation like achievement, recognition, responsibility, advancement, new experiences, being a necessary part of a winning team, and enjoyment of the work itself.

Sharpen your skills of managing and developing people. Pick the best. Let them know what is expected. Give them full opportunity to manage their territories and use their talents. Keep them constantly informed of how they are doing. Listen. Give the right assistance when and as it is needed. Reward them on the basis of results. And, have fun doing it!

If people are complex, and they are; if you'll be working with quite a variety, and you will; then perhaps the most important part of your job is to attempt to understand the needs of the people who report to you, and help those people meet their needs through the mechanism of productive work with your company.

Do that, and you are on the right track.

COACHING CHECKLIST

Do I(?), in my day-to-day coaching of sales representatives:
Stimulate results through my reps?

- Encourage their building of sales and developing themselves.
- Get a fix on the strengths and weaknesses of each rep to learn how to help them.
- Judge them on performance.

Set goals?

- Make them specific; to each person; clear and understood.
- Keep them up-to-date.
- High enough to require some "stretching."

Manage time wisely?

- Know where time is going.
- Cut back on unproductive aspects of the job.
- Help reps learn to manage their time.

Think before acting?

- Take time to think on important problems.
- Consult those involved or affected.

- Follow the steps of orderly thinking through the cycle of diagnosis.

Select the best?

- Continuously recruit for better qualified sales personnel.
- Develop specific requirements for each job.
- Use as many screens as practical to match job related behavioral characteristics of the candidate to the job specifications.

Train right the first time?

- Help reps develop their knowledge, attitudes, skills.
- Take the learner through preparation, presentation, application (doing), and follow through.
- Believe and implement "If the learner hasn't learned, I haven't taught."

Delegate effectively?

- Permit people to perform on their own.
- Encourage them to bring recommendations; not "problems."
- Delegate without "abdicating."

Convey knowledge of how they are doing?

- Provide timely praise and recognition for "jobs well done."
- Discipline reps when deserved in timely, appropriate manner.
- Discuss performance with each rep frequently, fairly, firmly, factually, friendly.

Give assistance when and as needed?

- Give timely review of reps' plans and sales strategies; *helping*, not telling.
- Encourage reps on difficult undertakings.
- Provide suggestions and assistance when needed.

Reward according to results?

- Reward, praise, and credit reps who produce results, without exception.
- See that promotions go to the best qualified subordinates—without exception.

Question, listen, and understand my sales reps?

- Find out the aspirations, ambitions, and motivations of each sales representative.
- Make skillful use of the seven tools of questioning and the seven tools of listening.
- Demonstrate a genuine concern for each rep.

Make contacts developmental?

- Try to make each contact a learning experience for each rep.
- Follow a schedule for developmental work-withs—even for the most seasoned veteran.
- Use all contacts to learn, teach, and make developmental.

Provide an atmosphere of two-way confidence?

- Develop an effective working relationship with each sales representative—no exceptions.
- Allow serious differences of opinion to be expressed without residue of hostility or anxiety.
- Have full confidence in subordinates. Make sure they know it.

Plan a sequence of developmental experiences?

- Plan *the next* one or two developmental experiences for each person to have.
- Provide at least two developmental experiences for each rep every six months.
- Have a mutually agreed upon plan of action for development with each person.

Use sales meetings as an effective training tool?

- Use at least a part of each group meeting for sales training, development, or coaching.
- Perfect my leadership skills using a variety of the methods shown to encourage participation, practice, and sharing (of goals, progress, techniques, and knowledge).
- Wrap up every meeting with commitment for follow through.

Make effective use of both formal and informal coaching?

- On work-withs, make notes and plans anticipating the next periodic coaching interview.
- In each annual coaching interview, plan follow-up action of an informal nature.

Consistently improve my own management skills?

- Make a conscious effort to improve upon my own listening skills.
- Keep up-to-date on sales management techniques.

Chapter Thirteen

Training Resources

A manager is expected to generate results by skillfully arranging and using all the resources which are available. Effectiveness is measured, of course, by what is accomplished through these resources rather than by what each manager personally does. One of the secrets of managerial effectiveness is based on awareness and proper use of available resources, and this secret applies directly to the training you provide your sales representatives.

This chapter presents guidelines for deciding whether to use outside training resources and, if you decide to, help in finding:

1. What kinds of resources are available.
2. Where can they be found.
3. How you might select them.

After reading this chapter, you should be in a better position to determine which resources among the many available alternatives will be most suitable for your particular needs and budget.

Before going any further, let's define "outside training resources." We mean all those resources, either personal or non-personal, which exist outside of your company. Quite possibly, you have a number of training resources within your organization which can be helpful to you. By all means, consider using them. But this chapter focuses on "external" people, materials, and services which you can secure in order to supplement and implement your overall sales training strategy.

At this point, we'll make several assumptions about your current situation: (1) you have some training need(s), and you know it; (2) you really aren't in a position to tackle all the training yourself; (3) you are looking for resources which will help you get the training job accomplished. If these assumptions fairly reflect your own thinking, then read on.

WHY CONSIDER OUTSIDE RESOURCES?

The question of whether you should even consider using outside training resources in the first place is not easily answered—there really are many answers. For a manager of salespeople, perhaps the most important answer is that you can expand your own managerial effectiveness through the use of outside training resources. With them you can add substance to your sales meetings, provide reminders to your people between meetings and field visits, help correct individual performance problems, and encourage professional development through self-study.

Another answer is that outside resources will enable you to get a training job done when: (1) such resources don't exist within your company; (2) your internal resources simply aren't available; or (3) internal resources cannot do the job for you on time. Outside resources can provide specialized help when it is needed, particularly when you have little time or experience to handle your sales training responsibilities entirely on your own. Outside resources can be used to help with specific parts of a training program and to supplement ongoing training programs.

Still another way to answer the question is to weigh the advantages and limitations of using outside assistance.

Advantages

Users of outside training resources gain a number of important advantages. These resources can provide:

1. Needed ability or expertise, when it isn't available within the company. Nowadays, it is possible to secure practically any specialized ability which may be lacking internally.
2. Needed professionalism, both in thoroughness of preparation and authenticity. This professional touch can add to your own credibility and lend support and emphasis to your management ideas.
3. Relief from time pressures, whether they arise from conflicting priorities or from suddenly occuring training needs. Many outside sources can provide you with suitable material and/or qualified people on short notice, if necessary.

4. Exposure to new ideas and to the thinking of others. This promotes a healthy interchange of ideas, and can help your salespeople become more aware of the universality of certain sales situations and problems.

5. Conservation of capital, as a viable alternative to putting a sales training specialist on the payroll or to investing in conference facilities and equipment.

6. Impetus for establishing ongoing sales training programs within the organization. Outside programs frequently become the foundation on which a company can build its own formal program.

Limitations

Of course, there are several limitations inherent in the use of outside resources. They stem primarily from the realization that you and your company can never totally relinquish the responsibility for training your salespeople; you, rather than the outside resources, will always have that ultimate responsibility. So be alert to these possible disadvantages:

1. Outside resources, by themselves, may lack continuity and permanence in relation to your overall training programs. You will need to supply the continuing emphasis.

2. Sometimes it's difficult to coordinate proper follow-through unless you do it yourself.

3. Short of hiring consultants for the purpose, field coaching by an outside resource is virtually impossible. That is something that only you can do.

4. Packaged programs are, of necessity, rather general in nature, and often cannot be precisely tailor-made for an individual sales force like yours. You need to translate the general principles into specific applications for your people.

5. If your salespeople use outside resources independently of you (for example, public seminars, correspondence courses), you can supervise them only indirectly, if at all.

Thus, as with most things, there are pros and cons to be considered before you decide to use outside training resources. On balance, it would seem that the advantages of expertise, variety, immediacy, and cost savings outweigh the possible disadvantages, particularly for a busy field sales manager like yourself. Nevertheless, a commitment to the use of outside assistance does imply an equal commitment to make certain the resources you select will be properly applied, both to help you get the training job accomplished effectively and to give you a fair return for your training investment. Your choice should be made only after careful consideration of the help you need in terms of its availability, qualifications, and limitations.

WHAT KIND OF OUTSIDE TRAINING RESOURCES ARE AVAILABLE?

Once you have decided to make use of outside training resources, you face a seemingly impossible task of selecting which one(s) will help you meet your objectives. The task is partly complicated by the wide variety and sheer quantity of available training resources; it may also be complicated by a vague or imprecise statement of your training objectives. Let's assume, however, that you have read an earlier chapter in this book and have developed clearly stated objectives for your group of sales representatives. All you need, then, is some guidance in sorting your way through the many resource options.

Printed Material

A number of outside training resources are available in print. They include a broad variety of books, periodicals, publications, programmed learning materials, and simulation games.

Books can provide excellent reference for managers, trainers, and salespeople alike. There are a great many books for managers and trainers which range from conducting effective sales meetings to solving individual performance problems in the field. They cover such topics as coaching and counseling techniques, group training techniques, training and developing professional salespeople and, more broadly, managing an entire sales force.

Similarly, there are a great many books which are aimed particularly at improving the skills and strategies of salespeople. They cover basic principles of salesmanship, use of psychology in persuasion and motivation, techniques of presenting and closing, profitable self-management, common selling mistakes, and many other related subjects. These books may be used for supplementary reference in training programs or for individualized self-development.

Periodicals provide another useful source of information and inspiration. Trade journals and industry newspapers can help salespeople learn and stay up-to-date with trends and developments occurring in their customers' industries. They can be useful in establishing your sales representatives as informed (and informative) sources of ideas for their customers. In addition to industry oriented periodicals, there are a number of magazines which focus on selling, salesmanship, and sales management. These can help salespeople to prepare themselves for dealing with certain kinds of sales situations or certain types of buyers and for solving many selling problems as they occur. Periodicals of this sort frequently provide a needed shot-in-the-arm for representatives who don't often see their managers in the field. They tend to be based on a sharing of experiences, which reassuringly reminds a person that others have faced and coped with situations very much like their own.

Publications (other than books and periodicals) can be useful to you as additional resources for training and developing your sales force. Some involve subscriptions to newsletters or information services. Others entail a series of motivational booklets or "reminder" messages. These can be effective supplements to your training efforts in much the same way as periodicals.

Still other publications provide tools for diagnosing sales behavior and for identifying strengths and weaknesses in interpersonal skills. These are generally accompanied by instructions and guidance for interpreting the results, so that both you and your representatives can know what adjustments are needed for greater on-the-job selling effectiveness.

Programmed learning materials are available in many forms, but one of the most basic and easiest to use is programmed instruction in printed form. Specially trained writers have prepared programmed texts in such subjects as fundamental selling skills, managing sales situations, and time and territory management.

Many companies accomplish product training and technical training through the use of programmed texts. Frequently, these are custom tailored to a company's needs, but occasionally there are "generic" programs which can fill a need with very little adaptation.

Programmed instruction can be an appealing alternative resource for many reasons: (1) the salesperson assumes responsibility for accomplishing the learning; (2) learning can take place at one's own pace without affecting other salespeople; (3) the manager's role shifts from teaching to measuring progress, counseling, and expanding on text materials; (4) material is standardized, which provides relief from tedious repetition (for the manager instructor) and ensures a consistent level of quality in the instruction; (5) it brings sales representatives up to a predetermined level of knowledge and competence at a relatively low total cost.

Simulations and games, another resource for aiding the learning process, often are available in printed form. They are generally designed so that participants can compete, individually and in teams, to achieve improved performance while learning concepts and practicing skills. A growing number of games are being developed especially for salespeople, and others designed for managers can be adapted to certain sales situations. Simulations and games offer the advantage of continuous and full involvement, relevance, practice in decision making, time compression, economy of operation and space, flexibility, and immediate availability.

Audiovisual Resources

If it seems that printed materials offer a multitude of possible resources for you, then you shouldn't be surprised to discover that audiovisual resources are plentiful, too. In fact, with television so well established as a communications medium (large screens, films in videocassette format, computer-assisted interactive video), the audiovisual field seems to be involved in continuous expansion and virtually unlimited technological advances. These resources include a wide selection of movie films, videocassettes, audiocassettes, sound slide programs, and other audiovisual materials which can be productively incorporated into your training activities.

Videocassettes are available for training and motivating salespeople. Some videos provide instruction and actual demonstrations of such fundamental selling skills as preparing presentations, handling objections, making telephone calls, improving personal organization, and closing. Others cover technical material, manufacturing processes, plant tours, and related industrial subjects.

Many videos now available can be used for motivational purposes; they frequently portray people who have excelled in some field of endeavor, and they convey tips for sales representatives on how they can excel in their chosen profession.

There are several reasons why you might prefer to use video films: (1) they are generally quite professionally done; (2) they can add excitement, motion, color, and realism to your training; (3) they are widely available and relatively low in cost, particularly on a rental basis; (4) they often are accompanied by helpful booklets with discussion guides, so that even a novice at training can obtain sound results from the use of videocassettes. These cassettes enable your sales force to study at home using videocassette players and their own television sets. Each sales rep can proceed at his or her own pace, stop and freeze-frame the tape, rewind, and replay parts for better understanding, and fast forward over familiar material, all for individualized study. These same features also allow you to better prepare your use of selected videocassette films in district meetings—you can select segments of the film for stopping, replaying, discussing, or reacting to during the meeting—a great way to get total involvement of your sales representatives.

Audiocassettes are an effective means of training salespeople. Many independent companies and producers are developing inexpensive training programs which are conveyed on audiocassettes, often in conjunction with a workbook. They can teach specific information, cover more general subjects, and deliver motivational messages. Tapes can either be borrowed from a commercial cassette library or purchased (often as a series) for use within a district or branch area. Audiocassettes offer low cost and convenience; salespeople can carry them with portable cassette players in the car, on the airplane, and in a briefcase.

Other audiovisual materials are available from numerous distributors and audiovisual manufacturers. They include prepared overhead transparencies, lecture notes, article reprints, and do-it-yourself kits.

Newer Technologies

Newer technologies have enhanced the adult learning process in recent years and are likely to become more prominent in the future. At this writing, their portability for use in the field is quite limited, so you may not find it realistic to consider these resources at the present time. On the other hand, if you have access to the appropriate equipment at your branch or sales office, you may be able to take advantage of these expanding technologies.

Computer Based Training (CBT) is a general term which covers computer assisted and computer managed learning, ranging from tutorials to dedicated training simulators. It is generally very effective for teaching knowledge that either doesn't change very much over time or requires memorization and repetition. CBT can employ a wide variety of media, including videodisks, CD ROM, hypertext, and the like. This technology makes it possible to create data-based learning systems which enable (1) managers and trainers to customize to individual needs, and (2) learners to self-pace their learning.

Interactive videodisk is often viewed as a separate and distinct technology, but it really is a special application of CBT. A single videodisk can offer up to 54,000 still images or up to 30 minutes of running video plus two audio channels. With this broad flexibility, interactive videodisk can be effectively used for visual demonstrations, skills development, and behavior modeling. Its use can range from brief presentations and (sales call) vignettes to full-blown demonstrations. One current application of this technology involves videotaping sales reps as they interact with videodisk programming; the tapes then become a tool for critiquing sales call behavior and coaching for improved skill application and performance.

Looking ahead, you can expect to see an emerging technology which involves the marriage of compact disk and interactive video technologies. Compact disk interactive (CDI) and digital video interactive (DVI) approaches are just in experimental or precommercial stages. Further out, you may even see hologram technology developed for applications in adult learning environments. For the present, however, newer technologies are likely to assume a more significant place in the array of training resources available to you.

Speakers

In addition to printed materials and audiovisual resources, you may want to consider the use of outside speakers in your training programs. Speakers can play a number of helpful roles in training salespersons: instructor, subject expert, sounding board, discussion leader, or motivator. Speakers frequently bring a fresh viewpoint, based on experience outside your own organization, that can both stimulate and inspire your sales representatives.

Speakers can also relieve you of the time-consuming aspects of preparing for productive sales training sessions. Some resource organizations simply maintain a speaker's bureau, while others are staffed to conduct complete workshops, seminars, and training meetings for their clients. Before you engage any speaker, you should first think through the role you want the speaker to play in your training program.

Outside Seminars and Courses

Still another available resource is an almost overwhelming number of public seminars and courses. Sponsored by a variety of organizations, universities, and associations, these courses offer two principal advantages: (1) exposure to highly qualified subject experts, and (2) an opportunity to exchange ideas and experiences with people from diverse industries. Such courses can be useful for addressing specific training needs of individual sales representatives; they can also be useful for expanding career possibilities and for longer term personal development.

Since there are so many outside seminars and courses available, you may want to consult with your personnel manager before making specific course selections for your people. In addition, you should determine that an outside seminar can be expected to meet specific training objectives for your people before you enroll them, that is, will it return more than its cost and the cost of time away from selling?

As you can readily see, there are many different kinds of outside training resources available. Your options are limited only by your imagination and by budgetary considerations. We can conclude that a tremendous amount of help is available if you want it and are willing to pay for it.

WHERE CAN OUTSIDE TRAINING RESOURCES BE FOUND?

Just as there are many kinds of resources, they can be found in a broad variety of places. Many of these sources will probably be familiar to you, and some may be new. Either way, these sources are frequently untapped and overlooked. We will mention them primarily as a reminder of the vast reservoir of assistance that exists for trainers of salespeople.

Public libraries are a good starting point for obtaining books, periodicals, and reference materials. They can help you identify and locate additional training resources. Many libraries have special reading programs, study groups, and other educational services. You may find suitable records, movie films, audiocassettes, and even projection and recording equipment. In addition, libraries often have meeting rooms available for groups the size of your sales force.

Public school systems frequently offer services which are little known or utilized. High schools may provide distributive education courses, ranging from basic salesmanship to supervisory and management training. Vocational, technical, and trade schools in your area can supply know-how and facilities which might fit in with your training needs. If these resources are limited, you may want to explore the possibility of extension services from your state department of education.

Intermediate education services, such as junior colleges or industrial education centers, may provide educational assistance in your community. Usually they offer two-year programs in such fields as applied science, arts, and engineering and serve as a good source of well-trained people for local industry. You can check these services for speakers, know-how, and educational materials.

Adult continuing education classes are conducted in many communities. Generally held in the evening, they provide opportunities for people to acquire and sharpen skills which can be useful on their jobs. Course instructors may also be available to supplement your training programs as speakers and subject experts.

Educational television stations, serving communities of all sizes, present programs for adults which may fill individual needs within your sales force. Skilled instructors and technical staff at these stations, well versed in the communicative arts, can also provide high quality counsel and assistance in training salespeople. You can check program listings of your local station, and contact their staff about participating in your training activities.

Colleges and universities offer a rich resource for business persons. A nearby institution may provide courses in business-related subjects, and may also encourage continuing study toward a degree for those who maintain full-time jobs. Of course, faculty members are professionally equipped to give both instruction and consultation; many of them welcome the opportunity to keep in touch with the business community.

University extension programs are tailored particularly to meet business needs. Many universities maintain extension programs not only on their campuses but also at extension centers in other communities. They combine direct mail and personal contact in order to make their educational services more widely available to business persons.

Financial institutions, such as banks, savings and loan associations, and insurance companies, can provide resources for training. Many of them offer excellent training materials which cover a wide range of sales-related subjects. Their officers may well be available as instructors, particularly in the fields of credit, finance, economics, accounting, and sales. Financial institutions in many communities will provide exceptional meeting facilities, as well.

Chambers of commerce, economic development councils, and boards of trade regularly sponsor sales conferences, management seminars, and short courses for executive development. They provide training in retailing, economics, and a variety of other subjects. You can contact an association's local office to determine what services can be supplied by its own staff or through its state and national offices.

Trade associations exist, broadly speaking, to serve their members' needs and purposes. One of their principal services is eucational and developmental in scope. You or your company no doubt belong to several major industrial associations whose services include conventions, clinics, seminars, correspondence courses, cassette programs, newsletters, and other similar sources of useful information. These organizations are often uniquely equipped, at local, state, and national levels, to assist with training sales and marketing people in your industry.

Professional societies and associations engage extensively in educational activities and services. Many people aren't aware of the broad range of high-quality programs which these organizations provide, and yet it is quite easy to get on their mailing lists. Many sponsor sales rallies, sales training clinics, and conventions on a local, regional, and national basis. Some publish books, pamphlets, and research reports which pertain to salesmanship and territory management. Local chapters can be an outstanding source for speakers, instructors, programs, seminars, and training courses.

Community agencies, such as YWCAs, YMCAs, Catholic Youth Organizations, and so on, frequently provide special educational services for adults. You can contact these agencies to determine whether their services would be suitable for your salespeople.

Government agencies, both state and federal, develop specialized training programs which are particularly helpful to business people. You can contact the U.S. Departments of Commerce, Labor, Agriculture, and Education, or their counterparts in your state. The Small Business Administration and the Government Printing Office provide useful printed materials on a broad range of business subjects.

Advertising agencies employ people with special creative talents that find useful application in preparing presentations, designing audiovisual aids for selling, and planning large and small meetings. You can draw upon these people to assist you with training your sales representatives in skills related to creative thinking, public speaking, making presentations, writing reports, and analyzing customer psychology.

Publishers, of course, generate a whole host of printed materials which are readily available as training resources. Since we have already mentioned these materials in some detail, we won't repeat them here. You may want to be on the lookout for major articles on training, training resources, and sales techniques as they appear in various periodicals. Publishers of these periodicals have fine reprint services that can fill important training needs. Certain publishing companies also supplement their line of printed materials with movies, videotapes, slides, cassettes, and supporting literature. You can tap these resources most effectively by securing catalogs from the key publishers in the sales, sales management, and sales training fields.

Correspondence schools provide a means for bringing education and training into the office and home on a highly individual basis. There are hundreds of these schools, and their courses cover an immense range of rather specialized subjects. Many are competent training organizations and well worth the time and money required. You may want to check a school's accreditation before you enroll your sales representatives.

Producers of audiovisual materials, like publishers, are a primary source of outside training assistance. They can assemble highly talented and eminent authorities in practically any field of endeavor and "deliver" them to your salespeople on film and/or tape at a very low cost. It is convenient and easy to get on these producers' mailing lists for catalogs and announcements of new releases. Their products and materials can be secured on loan, by rental, or by purchase.

Suppliers of goods and services usually can provide training assistance with special product, process, or equipment information. All you have to do is ask your company's suppliers whether they have training materials which would benefit your sales force. In addition, you can secure help from such suppliers as commercial artists, commercial printers, public relations firms, audiovisual equipment rental firms, hotels and conference centers, travel agents, and transportation firms. Your associates, friends, and acquaintances may have had successful experiences with some of these resources, so don't hesitate to ask them for recommendations and ideas.

Commercial training services run the gamut from selling a series of booklets or cassettes, on the one hand, to developing highly customized training modules for individual clients, on the other hand. Some services give either personal or correspondence training in nearly any subject you might need. Others focus their service on special fields such as speed reading, effective public speaking, personality development, sales technique, memory improvement, or personal success formulas. Some services apply their own special methodologies to the solution of particular training problems. There are many commercial training services which are eager to add companies like yours to their list of clients.

Professional consultants frequently are equipped to handle special training assignments or, at the very least, to recommend specialists for almost any training need. These specialists include individuals, associated professionals, and companies. Their capabilities vary from diagnosing sales performance problems, to instructing, and even to producing entire sales training programs (complete with audiovisuals, manuals, instructors, and evaluations). It will be worth your while to determine whether a consultant's capabilities and approach are compatible with your needs, your company policies and practices, and your budget for training.

In summary, outside training resources can be found practically anywhere and everywhere. This list of available sources is certainly not exhaustive, but it may serve to suggest the breadth of possibilities. Having identified a great many options, you now are in a position to make some sensible business decisions about which options you will pursue.

WHAT ARE USEFUL GUIDELINES FOR SELECTING OUTSIDE RESOURCES?

Your selection of various resources will involve considering and weighing several factors relating to needs, strategy, economy, efficiency, and effectiveness. You will find it helpful to think through your answers to questions like these:

1. Will the resource address the special needs of your sales force?
2. Will the methods and techniques taught by the resource be compatible with your own way of managing?
3. What will the resource cost in time, money, and effort?
4. Will the resource instruct efficiently?
5. Will the resource produce the desired results (Will it be effective)?

A number of subordinate questions may need to be considered when you make your selection. As you look them over, you can determine the relative importance of each one to your particular situation.

Objectives

Some of these questions relate to the objectives you have set for training. For example:

1. What will your people be expected to do differently (or better) after the resource has been used?
2. What do you want the training resource to accomplish, and how can the learning be measured?
3. Can the resource, in fact, accomplish what is needed?
4. What will the resource accomplish that present training and field coaching aren't accomplishing?

Scope, Content, and Adaptability

Thinking about other questions can help you assess the overall suitability of outside resources for training your particular group. These include:

1. Will the resource be used to supplement other training, or will it be used as the primary means of training your sales force?
2. Is the resource theoretical or practical in its approach?
3. Is the resource geared mainly for beginners in sales, for seasoned representatives, or does it relate to all levels of sales experience?
4. Does the resource simply provide instruction and focus on skill development, or can it also be expected to motivate salespeople and build esprit de corps?
5. Does the resource identify the learning objectives it is capable of accomplishing?
6. Is the content general, or is it rather specific to your industry or department?
7. Does the content differ in any significant way from the training provided in your company's internal resources?
8. Is it possible to preview the resource?
9. Can the resource be (pre)adapted to your situation, your industry, your products, your people, and your organizational environment?
10. Will your people respond favorably to the resource?

11. Will the resource address individual needs?
12. Can the resource be utilized in your representative's working environment?

Quality

Having considered various aspects of a resource's suitability for your purposes, you will want to consider its quality. It can be helpful to weigh questions such as these:

1. Has the resource been evaluated (by previous company use) for content, presentation, and effectiveness?
2. Who else has used the resource?
3. What have been the (measured) results?
4. Does the resource, or its marketer, have any proof of results and effectiveness?

Cost

Cost is an obvious factor, to be sure, but there can be several ways of getting at anticipated costs for outside training resources. For example:

1. How much time will be involved in using the resource?
2. Can the resource be available and ready when you need it?
3. How much time will you and your people need to invest in preparation, prework assignments, and follow-up work?
4. What will be the dollar cost, if any, for the resource?
5. What out-of-pocket expenses (for transportation, rooms, meals, shipping) will be incurred?
6. What will be the dollar investment on a per capita basis?
7. Will the cost be shared by others?
8. Are any performance guarantees (no work, no pay) offered by the resource?
9. Can you realistically afford the resource?
10. Can you obtain better value and cost effectiveness from another type of resource?

Measurement of Results

As a business person, you ultimately need to be interested in bottom-line results. As you assess various resources, you might focus your thinking on their potential effectiveness along the following lines:

1. What will be your return for the dollars, time, and effort invested in the resource?
2. What follow-up work will be required of you?
3. What, if any, provision for follow-up and continuing measurement is offered by the resource?
4. By what means will you monitor the effectiveness of an outside resource used independently by your people, without your direct involvement?
5. Will you be able to demonstrate, to your satisfaction and your manager's, that your use of the outside training resource contributes to bottom-line sales and profit results?

FOR FURTHER INFORMATION

The field of sales training has been and will continue to be enhanced by developments in the high technology communications area. Such technologies as videodiscs, satellite networks, and electronic trainers are expected to be used increasingly in the future. For purposes of this chapter, which is intended to focus on resources which a field manager can obtain with ease, we have chosen not to include details of the high technology resources.

Chambers of Commerce

Chamber of Commerce of the United States
1615 H Street, N.W.
Washington, DC 20036

Council of State Chambers of Commerce
Room 1018, 1028 Connecticut Avenue
Washington, DC 20036

Professional Societies and Associations

American Society for Training and Development
1640 Duke Street, Box 1443
Alexandria, VA 22313

National Society of Sales Training Executives
203 East Third Street
Sanford, FL 32771-1803
800-752-7613

Sales and Marketing Executives-International
380 Lexington Avenue
New York, NY 10017

Seminars

American Management Association
135 West 50th Street
New York, NY 10020

Dale Carnegie and Associates, Inc.
1475 Franklin Avenue
Garden City, NY 11530
516-248-5100

The Dartnell Institute of Management
4652 Ravenswood Avenue
Chicago, IL 60640

National Society of Sales Training Executives
203 East Third Street
Sanford, FL 32771-1803
800-752-7613

The Field Sales Manager's Most Important Questions upon Being Placed in a New Job

Personal strategy:

1. What do I need to learn quickly? How do I do it?
2. How do I identify and get reliable information I need? (How do I test its reliability?)
3. How should I allocate my time and other resources?
4. What will get me fired? What will get me promoted?
5. How much feedback do I give my boss?
6. What changes do I need to negotiate with my boss? With subordinates? With peers?
7. How do I identify points of diminishing return?
8. What external personal forces (family, social) affect my strategy? What internal (company) forces affect it?

My business objectives:

1. What is my mission in the organization?
2. What is critical that I personally do/do not do?
3. What are my key resources?
4. What are key *indicators* and *goals* of my performance?

The operation/organization/system:

1. What is the mission of the organization? What are its key *objectives*? (3–6 max.)

2. How does my function aid accomplishment of those objectives?
3. What external forces impact our organization?
4. What are our key resources and our unique competitive edge?
5. How are resources controlled?
6. What is acceptable standard deviation for performance?

Index

Also Available from Business One Irwin . . .

NEGOTIATING THE BIG SALE
Gerard I. Nierenberg

Let the "father of modern negotiating" show you how to build long-term selling relationships where everybody wins. Nierenberg shows you how to view bargaining as an ongoing process and gives you proven strategies for succeeding at the negotiating table.
ISBN: 1-55623-621-2

PERSONAL SELLING
How to Succeed in Sales
Charles Futrell

A practical, 10-step plan for conducting successful sales calls. Examples from companies like AT&T, General Mills, and Tupperware give you an easy-to-follow guide for building long-term relationships.
ISBN: 1-55623-651-4

COMPLETE GUIDE TO SALES FORCE COMPENSATION
How to Plan Salaries, Commissions, Bonuses, Quotas . . . Everything
Needed to Achieve Top Sales Results
James F. Carey

Design a plan that combines the best ideas for compensating the sales force with a realistic strategy that won't break the bank! This outstanding guide gives you the insight you need to design the perfect system for your company.
ISBN: 1-55623-696-4

NICHE SELLING
How to Find Your Customer in a Crowded Market
William T. Brooks

Gain the competitive advantage of "Application Selling" in today's highly competitive, crowded marketplace. This dynamic marketing tool gives you strategies for targeting customers, analyzing competitors, pricing, positioning, and capitalizing on personal selling opportunities.
ISBN: 1-55623-499-6

Available at fine bookstores and libraries everywhere.